D0432110

Making Candles & Potpourri

ILLUMINATE & INFUSE YOUR HOME

By Catherine Bardey

Photographs by Zeva Oelbaum

BLACK DOG
& LEVENTHAL
PUBLISHERS
NEW YORK

Copyright © 1999
Black Dog & Leventhal Publishers, Inc.

All rights reserved. No part of this book may be reproduced in
any form or by any electronic or mechanical means, including
information storage and retrieval systems without written
permission of the publisher.

Published by
Black Dog & Leventhal Publishers, Inc.
151 West 19th Street
New York, NY 10011

Distributed by Workman Publishing Company
708 Broadway
New York, NY 10003

Manufactured in the United States of America

ISBN 1-57912-076-8
h g f e d c b a

Design by 27.12 design, Ltd.
Studio photographs by Zeva Oelbaum

TABLE OF CONTENTS

PART I: *Making Candles*

PART II: *Making Potpourri*

Making Candles

History of Candles and Candle Making

Candles, one of the earliest sources of light, have played a crucial role in history. Without the precious flame to extend the daylight hours well into the night and to illuminate the halls of humanity, doctrines might not have been written, physicists on the brink of discovery might have befuddled their formulas in the dark and entertainment would have stopped at sunset. Evidence of candles, or of similar illuminating devices like torches and fire baskets, dates back to as early as 3000 BC. Over the centuries, candles have adorned the walls of rulers, played integral roles in religious ceremonies and lit streets and shops. Candles have even been used to keep time: In coal mines, less than half a century ago, candles marked with 12 lines—one for each hour—burned steadily to record work shifts.

Beeswax was one of the first ingredients used for making candles; recognized since ancient Roman times—and subsequently by many other civilizations—for its effective aromatic burning properties. (Beeswax burns very slowly and smells deliciously sweet.) The prohibitive cost of beeswax, though, greatly limited its use and availability; it became exclusively reserved for the wealthy and the Church. In thirteenth century England, beeswax became such a valuable and negotiable commodity that The English Tallow Chandlers and The Worshipful Company of Wax Chandlers were chartered to regulate and control the beeswax trade. Laws preventing the adulteration of the wax were passed and the penalties for breaking them quite stiff. Other candle making alternatives were sought, of which tallow (fat rendered from cattle and sheep) readily available in household kitchens, was the most common and least expensive. Unfortunately, candles made from tallow were messy to make, did not burn long, produced a lot of smoke and had an offensive odor. Spermaceti, the crystalline fat from the head of the sperm whale, and waxes extracted from plants and vegetables, were then success-

fully experimented with. Although these candles had resolved some of the unpleasant downsides of tallow, they were too difficult to produce on a large scale.

The nineteenth century produced major breakthroughs for the candle industry. With the discovery of stearin (or stearic acid) in 1823, a substance derived from treating tallow with alkali and sulfuric acid, candle quality was greatly improved. Stearin produced a hard and stable wax, which made for a less-smoky and brighter light. A few years later in 1825—and shortly before matches were invented in 1827—the first braided wick treated with mineral salts was used. The salt solution was instrumental in that it made the wick smoke less and caused it to curve during burning, thereby eliminating the nuisance of wick trimming.

The greatest advance for the candle making industry, however, came with the refinement of paraffin from crude petroleum in 1857. Paraffin, when combined with stearin, made for a clean-burning, long-lasting and odorless candle. The availability of this material at a low cost subsequently led to the invention of the first candle-making machine in 1834, a machine that could churn out 1,500 candles per hour. Today, candle manufacturers use similar tools and materials that

were used over a century and a half ago. They have further refined the process through the advent of recent wax-improving chemicals, thereby producing quasi-flawless candles.

Although electricity has replaced candles as the primary source of light, candle sales remain impressive. Few celebrations come to mind—birthdays, Halloween, or Christmas, for example—without the thought of flickering flames. Few romantic dinners are served without the seductive incandescent glow of a burning taper. And many of today's households have incorporated candles and the practice of burning candles into their décor, providing ambiance and atmosphere, comfort and character to a welcoming home.

With candle making kits and supplies readily available, more and more people re experimenting with and appreciating the craft of candle making as an outlet for creative energy, and as a way to embellish their surroundings. Some individuals explore the virtues of aromatherapy—the healing and soothing effect of certain scents—by incorporating essential oils in their ingredients; others recognize the value of a personalized candle as a decorative accessory and mood enhancer. Whatever the motivation may be, the art of candle making—while traditional in so many respects—undeniably lights the path to scenting and beautifying your home with innovation and flair.

CANDLE MAKING, IN A NUTSHELL

A candle needs four things to burn: fuel (wax), heat (flame), a connection between the fuel and the heat (the wick) and oxygen (so the flame will stay lit). When you're making candles, your possibilities for creativity are endless, as long as you can keep these four things (and some common sense) in mind. Basically, the steps to making candles are these:

1. Assemble your materials: wax, wicks and any additives you wish to use.

2. Prepare your wicks & molds: any priming or preparation that your method requires.

3. Melt the wax.

4. Form your candle: this step can be pouring, dipping or rolling, again depending on the method that you choose.

5. Let it dry and cool.

6. Trim the wick, clean up any rough edges.

7. Light your new candle and enjoy!

With a few exceptions, most of the tools and equipment you will need for making candles can be found in your kitchen cupboards. Whatever is missing can be purchased at any arts and crafts or candle supply store. (See page 170 for list of suppliers).

These are the tools that you will need regardless of the type of candle you choose to make.

- STAINLESS STEEL or ALUMINUM DOUBLE BOILER: for melting wax. If you don't have a double boiler, you can use an old stovetop pot, fill it half way with water and place a smaller pot in the center of it for the wax. To clean the double boiler after use, wipe away warm wax with paper towels. If you want to splurge, professional wax melting sets are readily available at craft supply stores.

- HOT WATER BATH: A large spaghetti pot and a couple of empty coffee or soup cans will do the trick. For a hot water bath, fill spaghetti pot one third of the way up with water and place on medium heat. Pour the melted wax into the cans and place them in the spaghetti pot to "stay warm" and melted. Hot water baths are essential when making hand-dipped candles.

- COOL WATER BATH: A cool-water bath is used for speeding up the wax drying process. Fill a spaghetti pot with cool water and place mold or container in water to cool down wax before unmolding. Essentially, your cool water bath (whether a bucket, pot or basin) only needs to be big enough to accommodate the size of your candle mold or taper.

- CANDY or WAX THERMOMETER: The thermometer must register readings of up to 300°F. The best kind to get is one that hooks onto the side of the pot—as opposed to one that sits on the bottom—so that the temperature reading is not affected by the heat source lying directly underneath the wax melter or pot.

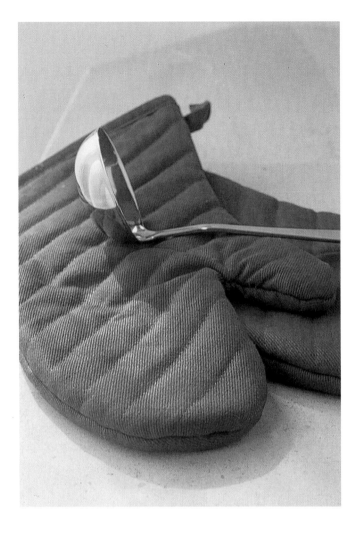

- HOT MITTS
  and RUBBER GLOVES: for
  holding pots and picking up
  hot items—molds, containers
  full of hot wax, etc. They also
  serve as protection against
  wax splashes.

- STAINLESS STEEL or
  GLASS PITCHER: for pouring melted wax into molds.

- VARIOUS TINS CANS
  (coffee cans, cans of peas,
  baking powder or baking soda
  cans, paint cans, large soup
  cans): for storing leftover
  wax and for holding wax
  when melting in the large
  spaghetti pot or double-boiler,
  or even for using as molds.

- SCISSORS and SHARP KNIFE: for trimming wicks and evening out bottoms of taper candles.

- PARING KNIFE: for removing seams from candles.

- MEASURING CUPS and SPOONS: for additives such as crystals and stearic acid.

- SCALE (optional): to calculate additives by percentage of wax content.

- GLASS DROPPER: for measuring fragrance and essential oils.

- MUSLIN CLOTH or TEA STRAINER (optional): for filtering dirt and debris out of soiled wax.

- HEAVY DUTY WAX PAPER or ALUMINUM FOIL: for covering and protecting work area.

- BAKING SODA: for putting out a flame in case of emergency.

- GRIDDLE or FLAT PAN: for evening out bottoms of block candles.

- PANTY HOSE: for buffing exterior of candles or removing mold seams.

- WAX REMOVING SOLVENT: for cleaning up hardened wax spills on counter tops and floors.

- OLD TOWELS and PAPER TOWELS: for cleaning up spills.

The Specialty Tools:

In addition to the basic tools, you'll need the following to accommodate the particular type of candle you will be making. Please note that no additional tools are needed for making rolled candles.

For making hand-dipped tapers:

- DIPPING VAT:
  Make your own out of an empty tennis ball can, juice can or tomato sauce can. When selecting a container, keep in mind that your actual taper or hand-dipped candle will be about two inches shorter than the length of the can. It is essential that the container used as a dipping vat can withstand the temperature of melted wax. Test it first by pouring boiling water into it to insure that the container is not affected by heat. Professional galvanized dipping vats are also available.

- DIPPING FRAME:
  These are essential for making multiple hand-dipped candles. (If you are making just one or two tapers, all you need is a place to hang the wick to let the wax dry between dips). Dipping frames are constructed in such a way that wicks are threaded onto both extremities of the frame—keeping the wicks taut—and so that more than one wick can be dipped in the wax at once. Dipping frames are available commercially or you can make your own (see below). Just make sure that your frame fits into the dipping vat.

- WICK HOLDER as an alternative to a dipping frame (see diagram A): You can construct a wick holder out of a piece of wood and some screw hooks. The only difference is that, unlike the dipping frame, wicks on a wick holder are not taut so candles may occasionally collide between dips. Choose a piece of wood that fits over the opening of the

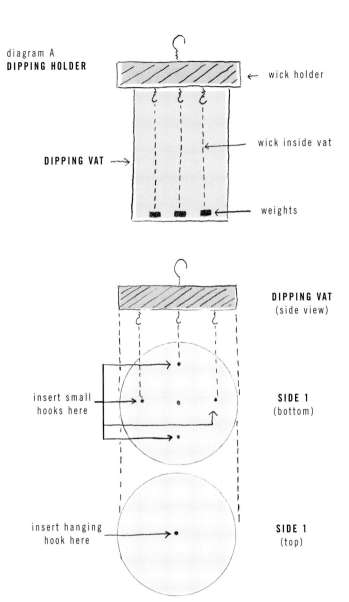

diagram A
DIPPING HOLDER

← wick holder

wick inside vat

DIPPING VAT →

weights

DIPPING VAT
(side view)

insert small
hooks here

SIDE 1
(bottom)

insert hanging
hook here

SIDE 1
(top)

dipping vat. On one side of the wood (bottom), screw in 4 to 6 screw hooks (depending on the size of the piece of wood and dipping vat) at equal distance from each other and equal distance from the center of the wood. On the other side (top), screw in another screw hook at the center. Thread wick through hooks on the bottom side. Thread a piece of string through hook on the top. This string should be hung on a nail so that the tapers can dry in between dips.

For Making Moldes and Poured Candles:

- MOLDS: The best molds to work with are made out of metal, rubber or plastic. Your selection will depend on the complexity of the candle, and the detail sought. Plastic or rubber molds (the polyurethane pop-out or rubber peel-out ones) provide more detail of the final product. Metal molds are generally used for making uniform, larger block candles. These are available in most craft supply and candle-making stores. You can also improvise with empty containers such as juice containers, soup cans, cookie dough tubes, PVC pipe tubes, seashells, eggshells and empty coconut shells. The only criteria for these improvised molds is that they must withstand the heat of melted wax. Basically, if you can pour boiling water into the improvised mold and it doesn't change shape or deteriorate, it can work as a candle mold. (See page 36 for more on molds.)

- TAPE or RUBBER BANDS: to hold two-piece plastic molds together, if necessary.

- WICK ROD or WICK HOLDER: for keeping the wick in place when the wax is hardening. You can improvise with a chopstick, pencil or piece of wire hanger that will suspend over the top of the mold or container (see diagram B).

- WICK TABS: little round metal circles that keep wire-core wicks in place when pouring melted wax into the container or votive. These are essential when when making smaller poured candles. They come in various sizes, depending on the size of wick you use and the size of the candle.

- A large container (BOX or BASIN) filled with sand (see page 66: for making sand molds).

- STAINLESS STEEL or RUBBER FUNNEL or a SMALL LADLE: for pouring wax into small molds

diagram B
WICK ROD (or holder)

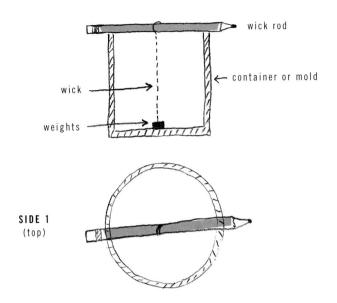

wick rod

container or mold

wick

weights

SIDE 1
(top)

For Making Votives or Hurricane Candles:

- WICK TABS: They keep the wick from moving in the container when the wax is poured. They come in different sizes which should be selected according to the size of the container.

- WICK ROD or WICK HOLDER: for keeping the wicks in place. Wick rods often come with professional votive molds but if you are improvising a pencil, chopstick or piece of hanger placed over the top of the molds will work as well. (See diagram C.)

- VOTIVE MOLDS: Ice cube trays work beautifully if you don't want to purchase a professional votive mold.

- SMALL LADLE: for pouring melted wax in votive molds.

diagram C
WICK ROD (chopstick)

wick

ice cube tray for making votives

Waxes

There are primarily two different types of waxes: paraffin wax and beeswax, each with its own specific characteristics and properties, each with its own melting point.

The melting point of a particular wax is the temperature at which the wax liquefies. The melting point of a particular kind of wax affects its pliability, hardness, durability and longevity. The higher the melting point, the harder the wax and the longer a candle will burn. Conversely, a wax with a low melting point (which liquefies at a lesser temperature) will not burn quite as long, but will be more pliable and malleable.

The kind of wax you use will depend on what kind of candle you're making. If you're making a hand-rolled candle, for example, you'll need a softer, more pliable wax that can be rolled easily and will not break. A wax with these characteristics (like beeswax) will have a relatively low melting point, which also means that candles made from this wax don't burn as long. On the other hand, if you're going to be making a molded candle using the pouring method, you'll want a wax with a higher melting point, that hardens well and burns for a long time.

Paraffin Wax

Paraffin wax is a chemical by-product of the petroleum industry. It is slightly translucent, odorless, hard and releases well from molds.

There are three different types of paraffin wax, defined primarily by its oil content. The result of this variance in oil content is that each wax has its own melting point: low, medium and high. The more oil the wax contains, the lower the melting point.

Paraffin waxes with low melting points (from approximately 125° to 130° F) are often called "container wax." The oil content is high which makes the wax softer, more pliable, sticky and burn faster. Container wax is primarily used for making container candles with the pouring method or hand-rolled pillars. Paraffin wax of this type is not recommended for making molded candles (where the mold is to be removed) because it tends to stick to molds, making it difficult to release the candle.

Paraffin waxes with medium melting points (from 130° to 145° F) work best for making free-standing pillars or molded candles (in which the mold is removed) using the pouring method, and hand-dipped tapers. This wax contains less oil than "container wax" which makes it harder, less sticky, and burn less quickly than wax with lower melting points.

Paraffin wax with higher melting points (145° F and over) has minimal oil content. This type of wax is hard, dries quickly and is ideal for making hand-dipped tapers. It also works well for over dipping (see page 54), a process which either colors the exterior of a candle, seals whatever decorations are fixed on the outside and makes them dripless.

Beeswax

Beeswax is a naturally sweet smelling, gold-colored wax that is extracted from beehives, cleaned and sometimes dyed. Beeswax is also long burning, soft, sticky and malleable. It comes in blocks or sheets, usually embedded with a lovely honeycomb design. Pure beeswax is ideal for making hand-rolled pillars and tapers. When making molded candles or hand-dipped tapers, beeswax should be blended with a hard paraffin wax for better results. Adding beeswax to paraffin will also lengthen the candle's burning time.

Beeswax in its pure form is not recommended for making molded candles because it is very sticky and makes the demolding process difficult.

NOTE: *If using pure beeswax in any mold, the temperature of the wax should not exceed 160° F as the wax will stick to the mold if poured at higher temperatures.*

POURING TEMPERATURES

SPECIAL TIP:

The temperature at which the wax should be when hand-dipped or poured is called "the pouring temperature." It varies with the type of candle made, and the kind of container used. (See page 34 for more information on molds.)

TYPE OF CANDLE/MOLD	POURING TEMPERATURE
Hand-dipped tapers	60° F (but increase last dip to 180° F for a smooth finish and sheen)
TRADITIONAL MOLDS	
Rubber	160° F – 180° F
Acrylic	180° F – 200° F
Plaster	160° F – 180° F
Metal	180° F – 200° F
NON-TRADITIONAL MOLDS	
Glass	160° F – 200° F
Clay	180° F – 200° F
Foil	180° F – 200° F
Cardboard	160° F
Sand	280° F (for the sand to stay on)
	160° F (for the sand to come off)
Plastic	160° F

The wick is essential in making a candle burn, and burn well: It connects the wax to the flame, thereby connecting the candle's fuel (the wax) to the heat source (the flame).

A wick works more effectively when it is primed, a simple process by which the wick is dipped into melted wax before use, dried, dipped again and dried. The purpose of this process is to remove air bubbles possibly trapped in the wick so that the wick burns smoothly, to make it completely moisture proof and to enable the wick to light easily. Priming is not crucial to the candle making process, but it's a good habit to get into and takes very little time.

Wicks are made out of woven cotton threads that have been treated with a chemical fire-retardant solution so that they burn slowly and decompose as they burn. Like waxes, wicks come in a variety of shapes and sizes, and some woven are more tightly than others. The type of wick you select will depend on the type of candle you are making. There are essentially three types of wick: square-braided, wire-core, and flat-braided wicks.

Square-braided wicks:

- Square-braided wicks are used primarily for making large mold or block candles and pillars. They come in numbered sizes, from 1 (the thinnest) through 10 (the fattest). The fatter the candle, the fatter the wick used.

Wire-core wicks:

- Wire-core wicks have wire in the center, which makes them stiff. Wire wicks are thus able to stand pretty much on their own, or in a pool of melted wax. This property makes them ideal for votives, container and sand candles. They usually come in three sizes: small, medium and large.

Flat-braided wicks:

- Flat-braided wicks, which look like flat pieces of string, are used primarily for hand-dipped tapers or small pillar candles. They come in different sizes that are determined by the number of strands in the wick. The bigger the wick size, the higher the number of strands and the fatter the wick. Sizes range form extra small (15 ply or 15 strands) to extra large (60 ply or 60 strands). Smaller candles require

wicks that are smaller, hence, with fewer plies.

Wick tab or holder:

- A wick tab is a little piece of metal with a hole in the center of it, sometimes with little teeth, through which a wick is threaded and held in place. Wick tabs hold the wick at the bottom of a mold or container to keep the wick in place and standing up straight when the wax is poured.

Additives:

Additives are blended into wax to give it certain properties such as increasing its burning time, making it harder and brighter, lowering the melting point or facilitating mold release. Other additives, such as dyes and essential oils, can be used to enhance appearance and aroma and create an atmosphere.

- LUSTER CRYSTALS: They harden the wax of any candle and will lengthen its burning time by raising the wax's melting point. These crystals will improve a candle's luster, make white candles whiter and brighten colored ones. Use 1 tablespoon per pound of wax. Melt it first in a little bit of the wax before adding to the bulk of melted wax.

- CLEAR CRYSTALS: In addition to lengthening a candle's burning time, they help eliminate air bubbles on the surface

of the wax, brighten color and make tapers dripless when overdipped in a high clear crystal content wax. Use 1 tablespoon per pound of wax. For overdipping purposes, use 1 cup per pound of wax.

- STEARIC ACID (or stearin): A fatty acid whose purpose is to harden the wax and lengthen its overall burning time. Stearic acid also causes wax to shrink slightly, thus making it easier to remove the candle form the mold. It should be used sparingly at about 3 to 5 tablespoons per pound of wax. Melt it first in a little bit of the wax before adding it to the bulk of melted wax. Note: do not use stearic acid with plastic or rubber molds as the acid will eat through the mold.

- MICROCRYSTALLINE WAXES: there are different types of microcrystalline waxes available, each with its own set of properties. Some make wax less brittle, others increase the glow or make wax stickier. The type of microcrystalline wax you will use depends on the property you are looking for. Check with your candle supply store for which type best suits your needs.

- WAX DYES: these can be melted into the wax directly, or melted into one of the above additives before being poured into the rest of the wax. Wax dyes usually come in disks or squares, and you'll need about one disk per pound of wax. A less traditional method for dying wax is by using crayons of which you'll need between 5 and 10—depending on the desired shade—per pound of

wax. Keep in mind that color will lighten as the wax cools and hardens.

- CANDLE SCENTS: candle scents, specifically used for scenting candles, come in liquid or solid form, and a little usually goes a long way. Essential oils and fragrance oils are also very effective as a way to scent wax. (See Essential Oils Chart page 154). Use 4 to 5 drops per pound of wax.

- MOLD-RELEASE SPRAY: Mold-release spray or silicon spray is the equivalent to non-stick vegetable spray for cooking. While not crucial to the candle-making process, it will certainly make unmolding candles, especially ones made in special tin containers, an easier process. Always use mold-release spray when making candles with beeswax.

- MOLD SEALER: A mold sealer is a reusable rubbery substance that sticks to wax and helps seal wick openings at the bottom of molds or containers to prevent melted wax from leaking after it is poured.

Molds and containers give your candles character. Depending on your mood and the effect you are trying to achieve, you can go with a classic, more traditional look, like a pillar candle, or opt for something more creative and less structured like a candle in a walnut shell that floats. Whatever you chose, experimenting is half the fun. You might even surprise yourself with how far you can go!

There are essentially two types of molds: commercial candle-making molds available at any arts and crafts store or candle-making supplier (see list on page 170), and molds that are not necessarily intended to be candle molds but that work anyway. Either way, these molds should be clean and dry before use, and sprayed with mold release or silicon spray.

Professional candle-making molds come in various shapes and sizes, and in different materials. Molds can be made out of metal, rubber, plastic, latex, acrylic, sometimes glass and are reusable. Some molds are one-piece and these are for shapes in which the opening of the mold is wide enough so that the candle comes out. Others are made out of two of more pieces that are held together. Two or multiple-piece molds are for making more complicated candles like figurines or convoluted shapes for which the mold needs to be opened or pulled apart for the candle to be taken out. Some molds have seams and others don't. There are pop-out molds and peel-off molds made out of durable plastic, acrylic or rubber in which the wax is poured; the mold is then literally peeled off the candle once it is dry. Some molds are very ornate to create detail on the candle's surface, other molds are very simple and plain. Whatever mold you select will depend on the mood you're in, the type of candle you want to make and your budget. Regardless, all commercial candle-making molds come with care and wicking instructions, as well as precautions. Follow them carefully.

Molds that are not necessarily intended to be candle molds but work anyway can be divided into two groups: the disposable kind and the non-disposable kind.

Non-disposable molds are containers like coffee or soup cans, clay flower pots, ice cube trays or cupcake pans (for making votives), candy molds and basically any container that can withstand the heat of melted wax and that has an opening wide enough so that the candle can be removed. These molds can be re-used over and over again.

Disposable molds can be found pretty much anywhere you look around: a sturdy ice cream carton, a wax coated frozen juice can, a wax coated yogurt container or Dixie™ cup, a piece of aluminum foil shaped into a nest, a glass baby food jar, a plastic cream cheese container, or even a sand filled box in which wax is poured (see page 66 for more on sand candles). Once again, the only caveat with a disposable mold is that the container can withstand the heat of melted wax. If you're not sure, test the container first by pouring a little bit of wax at the bottom of it and see what happens. What distinguishes these molds from the other non-disposable molds is that these are used once. The glass, carton, cardboard or foil is peeled away or broken off after the wax has hardened and cooled.

CONTAINERS

Containers referred to here are for making container candles in which the wax stays in the container and the container is part of the presentation. These containers therefore do not have to be sprayed with mold-release or silicone spray, but they do need to be clean and dry prior to use. Most of these containers can also be used as molds for making molded candles, by spraying them with mold-release gel and pulling out the finished candle or breaking the mold.

Some containers, like molds, can be used more than once; others are for single use only. With the exception of making sure that the container can withstand the heat of melted wax, the only limit to what kind of container you can use is your imagination. From household items like teacups or flowerpots to things you'd find in nature, like eggshells or baby pumpkins, the possibilities are truly endless.

Here are a few ideas to get you started—but truly, you can use just about anything

TEA TIN

SOUP CAN

CLAY FLOWERPOT

JUICE GLASS

ICE CUBE TRAYS

SMALL DECORATIVE BOWLS

TEACUPS

COFFEE MUGS

A GALVANIZED BUCKET

CUSTARD CUPS OR RAMEKINS

SUGAR BOWL

JAM JAR

Single-use containers can be made out of virtually anything. Often, you'll find things in nature (or more realistically, the grocery store) that you want to use—there are two ways you can go with this. For a special occasion, you can make a truly "one-time use" out of a piece of fruit, an arrangement of fresh flowers or anything else that will hold a candle but might spoil. In these situations, when your elements start to wilt, it's over. On the other hand, if you'd like your candle to last a little longer, you can use a container that may not stand up to a refill once the candle burns down, but will hold up as long as the wick does.

Again, this list is just to get you started–
let your imagination go wild!

- EMPTY SQUASH
- BABY PUMPKIN *(semi-perishable: this will last a few weeks)*
- EGGSHELL
- WALNUT SHELL
- CLAM, MUSSEL OR SCALLOP SHELL
- HALF A COCONUT SHELL
- SMALL GOURD
- HOLLOWED-OUT APPLE OR PEAR
(perishable: this is pretty, but will only last one night)

With containers like these, be sure that they're clean and dry before you pour the wax. Hollow them out thoroughly and keep an eye on the perishable ones. You will find that the more you experiment with candle making, the more ideas you will come up with. Pretty soon, every time you'll look at something, you'll wonder what kind of candle it would make!

Customizing and giving your candle character is a tremendously fun aspect of candle making. The more you do it, the more you realize that there are endless ways to decorate your candles, from hand-carving to applying decals and dried leaves, from adding grapefruit oil, orchid fragrance or ground cinnamon, to adding lemon rinds in the wax itself.

The custom process begins at the point when the wax is melting—before pouring, casting or hand-dipping the candle—by adding scents and color. Candles can also be decorated after the candle is finished by applying items to its exterior or carving designs in the outer layer of the hardened wax.

Scents

There are a variety of ingredients with which you can scent your candle: commercial candle making scents, fragrance oils, essential oils or fragrant ingredients—such as herbs and spices. No matter what you use, you'll add it to the melted wax before it is poured.

Commercial candle making scents come in liquid form and are available through candle making suppliers and most arts and crafts stores. Scent strength varies from one manufacturer to the next, so follow directions on the bottle for dosage. An approximate amount is about 1 ounce of liquid scent for 2 pounds of melted wax.

Fragrance oils are laboratory made oils that are 100% synthetic. They are available in many health food stores and specialty and fragrance shops. The array of scents ranges from scents that you would find in nature like rose or lilac or vanilla bean, to more abstract aromas like that of freshly mowed grass or cotton candy. Although these fragrance oils are technically not intended for scenting candles, most of them do quite well. The only thing to remember is that they are highly concentrated, so a little goes a very long way. An approximate dose is about 10-15 drops per pound of melted wax.

Essential oils are natural oils derived from plants or parts of plants, and these oils serve a dual purpose: they smell good and they have therapeutic properties such as calming, rejuvenating, healing or soothing. Like fragrance oils, essential oils are available in most health

food stores and specialty shops. Some essential oils mix with wax better than others. If you have time, a trial run is recommended: Pour a little bit of the melted wax in a Dixie™ cup, add a few drops of essential oil, let the wax cool and harden and assess the results. The dosage for essential oils is the same as for fragrance oils: add 10-15 drops of oil per pound of melted wax.

Natural ingredients, crushed or powdered, are another effective way of scenting your candle. These ingredients will also add color and a bit of texture to the wax. Ground cinnamon, crushed lavender flowers, finely ground lemon zest, or ground cumin for example, adds a wonderful aroma to the candle. These ingredients may lodge themselves towards the bottom of the candle, which actually gives it an appealing look. Use them sparingly, though, as too much ingredient could interfere with the wax hardening process and the way the wick burns. You don't want to end up with big globs of stuff floating around in the pool of melted wax by the wick. About 1 teaspoon of any ground herb or spice per pound of wax will work.

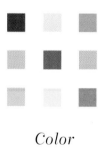

Color

B eyond the natural ingredients, there are a variety of ways that you can make your candles come alive with color. Candle dyes come in blocks (find them at candle supply or art stores), and can sometimes be found in powdered form. You can also use grated crayons, spices, even food coloring (although it's not ideal). For the highest degree of control, you should melt your dye separately from the wax, then add slowly, stirring constantly. If you're using a crayon, spice or other coloring agent, mix it with a separate amount of melted wax and add it to your main wax—AFTER you've mixed in any additives or fragrance.

Many things can be done to a candle after it is complete: over-dipping, carving and exterior collage are just a few examples.

Over-dipping

Over-dipping is a process by which the candle is dipped one last time into wax for a "final" layer. The purpose of over-dipping is two-fold: One is to give it certain qualities such as making it dripless or giving the outer layer a smooth and hard finish, the other is for engraving the candle or giving white candles a colorful and glowing outer shell. A candle should be over-dipped when it is hard but still warm to the touch. For making the candle dripless or hardening its finish, use a wax with a higher melting point than the wax used for making the candle. This will create a hard outer shell around the candle, which will protect the candle. It will also keep it from dripping because the hard shell will contain the melted wax close to the wick. Melt a small amount of the wax and mix in the appropriate amount of clear crystals or additives (see page 32 for additives). Dip the candle into the wax one to three times, allowing wax to dry in between dips.

For coloring a white candle, add dye to the wax and dip one to four times depending on the shade you wants, allowing the wax to dry in between dips. For added effect, cover part of the candle with tape, stickers or paper before the dips. When you remove the piece of tape or sticker after dipping, it will expose the color of the candle underneath.

Carving

Once your candle is overdipped, you can go one step further by using a sharp object such as a knife or the end of a paper clip to scrape off parts of the colored outer layer, exposing the white or colored candle underneath. You can play around with layers of color by over dipping in different colored waxes, exposing one color or another depending on how deep the engraving on the shell.

Exterior Collage

Decorating through collage is a lot of fun and extremely easy. Essentially, you can make anything stick on the outer layer of a candle by "gluing" it on. Melt a small amount of high melting point paraffin. Use a brush to apply the melted wax to the part of the candle on which you want to glue something. If you are placing decals, leaves or pressed flowers on the shell, then brush over the item once it has been affixed to the shell to give it a smooth surface.

The types of things that can be glued to candles are endless. The following is only the beginning of a list of examples:

- CINNAMON STICKS
- DRIED FLOWERS, HERBS AND LEAVES
- VERY THINLY SLICED DRIED FRUIT
- CAKE DECORATIONS SUCH AS SPRINKLES AND SUGAR CRYSTALS
- DECALS
- SPARKLES AND GOLD DUST
- STICKERS
- VANILLA BEANS
- COFFEE BEANS
- SEASHELLS
- SAND
- BEADS
- SEQUINS

NOTE: *It's best to use larger, pillar type candles for decorating in this fashion as the decorations will be less likely to interfere with the wick and candle burning process. It's also a good idea to periodically clean out resulting debris in the wax pool.*

Other Ideas

- Push a small trinket halfway in the melted wax of your mold to make a treasure candle.

- Shave bits of old colored candles with a cheese grater or vegetable peeler and add the colored shavings to a glass with a wick/wick tab in it. Compress the shavings firmly in the glass and around the wick. Continue adding shavings until the glass is full.

- Roll a warm pillar candle in ground spices, crushed herbs and dried flowers, or glitter.

- Roll a warm pillar candle in a piece of corrugated cardboard for a rustic look.

- Chop pieces of colored leftover wax into chunks and place in a mold. Pour clear wax over the chunks to make a chunk candle.

- Using acrylic paint, stencil, handpaint or sponge designs onto your candle.

Recipes & Techniques

Hand-dipping is the oldest, most traditional method for making candles. Hand-dipped tapers are elegant and simple, and require very little equipment.

The process basically consists of building up layers of wax on a wick. The wick is repeatedly dipped into a vat containing melted wax. Between each dip, the wax hardens so that the next layer of wax will stick to it. It takes anywhere from 30 to 40 dips to make a standard size taper, one that will fit into a candlestick.

There are three ways of dipping candles. The first is by using a professional dipping frame, available through candle-making suppliers. The wick is threaded through the frame and pulled taut. The second is by fabricating a wick holder (see diagram page 21) and using a can (metal tennis ball can, soup can, coffee can) to hold the melted wax. The height of the vat will determine the length of the candle. After threading the wicks and attaching them to the screw hooks, the bottom of the wicks must be weighed down. You can purchase candle weights that are specifically made to attach to the bottom of the wick, or you can improvise by using a nut, bolt, cooking weight, fishing weight or any small object that is heavy and that can be easily attached. The third way of making hand-dipped tapers is extremely simple and doesn't require any dipping frame or wick holder. You simply hold the wick by the tip when dipping it into the vat or can of melted wax, and then you attach the wick to a hanger or clothes line to let the wax dry between dips. Make sure you cut the wick long enough so that it can be attached to something. This method is particularly effective for making smaller tapers like birthday candles. Many hand-dipped tapers are made in pairs, where one end of the wick is dipped, then the other end is dipped, after the first end has cooled. You've probably seen pairs of hand-dipped tapers that are connected by a single wick; they are either dipped in this way or on a dipping frame where the wick can remain a continuous thread.

The type of wax you should use is one with a medium melting point, to which beeswax, additives, dyes and scents and can be added. You can also use 100 % pure beeswax for the whole taper. The amount of wax needed depends on the size of the vat or container that holding the melted wax. Use the procedure on page 60 to figure out how many pounds of solid wax you will need to melt to fill your vat. For successful dipping, the melted wax should be between 155° F and 160 F, and approximately 160° F to 165° F if using pure beeswax or a paraffin–beeswax blend. If the temperature is too low, the wax will stick unevenly to the layers and look clumpy. If the wax is too hot, the wax layers will melt when they are re-dipped. Use hot or cool water baths to adjust the temperature of the melted wax when necessary. After you have finished dipping, the container should be half filled with leftover wax. This wax can be reused. Use a medium sized, flat-braided wick, and remember to leave some extra wick for attaching to the wick holder.

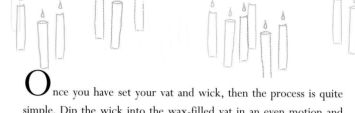

Once you have set your vat and wick, then the process is quite simple. Dip the wick into the wax-filled vat in an even motion and hold in the wax for about 2 to 3 seconds. Remove the wick in a slow even motion and allow to dry for 3 to 5 minutes. Repeat the process for 30 to 40 dips until the desired thickness for the top of the candle is reached.

Giving the hand-dipped candle its tapered appearance (wider at the bottom and gradually narrower as it reaches the wick) is part of the dipping process. Once the candle has reached the desired thickness towards the wick, then less of the candle is dipped in the dipping vat for the next set of dips. Once the top third of the candle has reached the desired width, then less of the candle is dipped during the next set of dips, and so on. For the last few dips, only the last quarter of the candle should be dipped in wax to ensure that the bottom is the thickest part of the candle.

For the very last dip, heat the wax to 180° F. This will give the candle a smooth finish. At this point, the tapers can be overdipped (see overdipping process page 46) for carving or color. Once the last layer of the candle is dry but the wax is still a bit warm, trim the wick at the top leaving at least one inch of extra wick. Trim the bottom of the candle and place it briefly on a heated skillet or frying pan to even out the surface. Let tapers dry for at least one hour.

RECIPE FOR MAKING BASIC TAPERS WITH A PARAFFIN/BEESWAX BLEND

Ingredients:

- MEDIUM MELTING POINT PARAFFIN WAX (50% OF TOTAL WAX WEIGHT)
- BEESWAX (45% OF TOTAL WAX WEIGHT)
- STEARIC ACID (5% OF TOTAL WAX WEIGHT)
- 1 DYE DISK PER POUND OF WAX
- 5 DROPS OF ESSENTIAL OR FRAGRANCE OIL PER POUND OF WAX

Equipment:

- DOUBLE BOILER
- DIPPING VAT OR CONTAINER
- DIPPING FRAME OR WICK HOLDER
- MEDIUM SIZE FLAT-BRAIDED WICK (24 TO 30-PLY)
- SCISSORS FOR CUTTING THE WICK
- SHARP KNIFE FOR TRIMMING THE BOTTOM OF THE TAPERS
- SKILLET OR FRYING PAN (OPTIONAL) FOR EVENING OUT THE BOTTOM OF THE TAPER

- Assemble wick frame according to manufacturer's directions or make your own.
- Melt wax to 160° F – 165° F
- Add stearic acid, dyes, and fragrance
- Dip wicks slowly and evenly in melted wax and wait 3 seconds; remove wick from wax and allow to dry (3 to 5 minutes). Continue dipping wicks (between 30 and 40 dips, depending on the desired thickness) allowing wax to dry between layers, keeping in mind the tapering method mentioned above
- Heat wax to 180° F for final dip . After final layer has dried, trim top of wicks (leaving at least 1 inch) and bottom of candle and flatten on a heated skillet or frying pan for a leveled surface

T he Pouring Method is a simple technique for making pillar, molded or container candles.

There are three basic steps to the Pouring Method:

1) SELECTING AND PREPARING THE MOLD AND WICK

2) PREPARING AND MELTING THE WAX

3) POURING THE WAX INTO THE MOLD AND
LETTING IT COOL DOWN

1. Selecting and Preparing the Mold and Wick

T here are hundreds of molds and containers available for making candles (see page 34 for mold ideas). The type of mold or container you choose will depend on the effect and look you want to give your candle. Whether using a traditional mold or something a little more abstract like a pumpkin or clay flower pot, the methods by which the mold/container and wick are to be prepared remain similar.

If using a professional candle making mold, make sure the mold is clean and dry, spray the inside of the mold with mold release or silicone spray. Thread the wick according to manufacturer's instructions.

If using an improvised container or one that is more than 2 inches in deep (a coffee can or soup can, for example) there are two ways of threading the mold.

METHOD ONE:

- *Drill a tiny hole in the center of the bottom of the can.*
- *Make a knot at one end of the wick and thread it through the hole at the bottom.*
- *Pull the wick through to the top of the mold so that it is taught, and attach that end to a wick rod (a pencil, chopstick, or piece of wire) which will be rested on top of the edges of the container. The wick rod keeps the wick taut and centered as the wax cools. Make sure you use mold sealer on the exterior of the can where the hole is so that there are no leaks.*

METHOD TWO:

- *Attach the wick to a wick tab by inserting the wick through the hole in the tab and clasping it tight with pliers.*
- *Place the wick tab at the bottom of the container and anchor it in the mold by pouring a thin layer of melted wax at the bottom of the container (1/4 to 1/2 inch of wax should suffice)*
- *Pull wick through to the top of the container.*
- *attach loose end to the wick rod and rest it on top of the container's edges.*
- *Make sure the wick is taught enough so that there is no slack, but not so taught that the wick tab can't resting at the bottom of the container.*
- *Use this method when making sand candles.*

If using a shallow improvised container that is less than 2 inches deep (votive molds, seashell, eggshell, walnut shell, coconut shell), clasp a wire-core wick onto a wick tab, and place the wick at the bottom of the mold.

Depending on the depth of the container, you might want to wrap the other end of the wire-core wick around a wick rod and rest it on top of the container.

2. *Selecting, Preparing and Melting the Wax*

The type of wax you select for the pouring method depends on the kind of molded or poured candle you want to make. Use paraffin wax with a low melting point for making container candles; paraffin wax with a medium melting point for making molded candles; and paraffin wax with a high melting point for making votives, or small container candles.

Whatever wax you use should be clean and debris-free. If you are using recycled wax from bits and pieces of leftover candles, be sure to melt the wax beforehand and strain it through a cheesecloth or strainer to remove extraneous material.

The amount of wax you will need depends on the size of the container or mold used. To determine this amount, fill the mold directly with water, or use a plastic bag if you want the mold to stay dry. Pour the water out into a measuring cup to determine its liquid volume in fluid ounces or cups. Convert the liquid volume into pounds by referring to the chart below.

LIQUID VOLUME	EQUIVALENT IN POUNDS OF WAX
6 fluid ounces or 3/4 cup	1/2 pound solid wax
12 fluid ounces or 1–1/2 cup	1 pound of solid wax
24 fluid ounces or 3 cups	2 pounds of solid wax

The temperature of the wax is an important element in the wax melting process. There are three measuring points that correspond to three different stages of the melting process: the melting point, the pouring temperature and the flash point.

The melting point is the temperature at which wax melts. Different waxes have different melting points. The higher the melting point, the harder the wax and the longer the candle will burn. The melting point of a wax does not actually need to be monitored during the melting process. However, knowing what a melting point represents comes in handy when purchasing wax, which is usually identified by its melting point.

The pouring temperature is the temperature at which the wax should be when it is poured into the container or mold. This is the temperature that needs to be monitored by a wax or candy thermometer. The pouring temperature will vary, depending on the mold or container used. Getting the temperature right is crucial to the appearance of the final product. If the wax is too cold when poured, the candle could end up with air bubbles in it, or the surface of the candle may be "frosted," which means it has a whitish exterior. If the wax is poured too hot, it can damage the mold or container, or make the candle difficult to unmold. Keep an eye on the thermometer. If the wax gets too hot, it can always be cooled by immersing the melted wax container in a cool water bath. For pouring temperatures see chart in "Special Tips" section of Basic Ingredients on page 29.

NOTE: *Pure beeswax should never be poured at a temperature above 160° F. Exceeding this temperature would cause the wax to stick to the mold.*

The flash point is the temperature at which wax will ignite. A few degrees can make all the difference and turn your melted mass into a blazing inferno. Always keep in mind a wax's melting point when monitoring the pouring temperature. If the wax gets too hot, lower its temperature by placing it in a cool water bath.

TYPE OF PARAFFIN	MELTING POINT	FLASH POINT
low melting point	125° F – 132° F	around 405° F
medium melting point	132° F – 145° F	around 450° F
high melting point	145° F – 150° F	around 475° F

3. Pouring the Wax Into the Mold and Letting it Cool Down

When the mold and wick are ready and the wax is at the right pouring temperature, the last step—pouring the wax into the mold or container—is just a matter of exercising caution and common sense.

First, be sure to transfer the melted wax from the double boiler into a pitcher with a pourable spout. This will make pouring into the mouth of the mold or container a lot easier. Use an oven mitt to pick up the double boiler as the handle is certain to be very hot. Transfer the liquid over some newspaper so as to avoid wax splashes in the work area. If the mouth of the mold or container is too small, use a funnel or small ladle to fill the cavities.

Once the mold is filled, the wax needs to cool down before the candle can be removed. The cooling down process can be facilitated with the use of a cool water bath in which the mold is placed. When putting the mold into the cool water bath, make sure that the water doesn't splash into the mold and wax. No matter how impatient you are about seeing your final product, remember to use cool water, not cold water. The cooling down process is a gradual one. Cooling the wax too quickly may cause the appearance of air bubbles, air holes or cracks in the candle.

The wax now cool, the candle can be removed from its mold. Once the candle is removed, the surface can be buffed and marks from mold seams evened out. Simply use a piece of panty hose and rub it on the surface of the candle until smooth.

If the candle comes out with an uneven bottom and wobbles, heat a skillet or griddle and briefly place the bottom of the candle on the pan to slightly melt the exterior. Press candle on a flat surface and allow to dry.

Basic Votive Receipe

Votives can be displayed on their own, in a favorite votive container, or inside a hallowed pumpkin. They can also be placed in a small glass and tucked in a paper lunch bag for a fun effect at a summer evening picnic. They are usually made in bunches of six or eight and take little time to make.

Ingredients

2 POUNDS PARAFFIN WAX WITH A

LOW MELTING POINT

5 TABLESPOON STEARIC ACID

2 TABLESPOONS LUSTER CRYSTALS

8 DROPS ESSENTIAL OIL OF YOUR CHOICE

DYE, IF DESIRED

Equipment

DOUBLE BOILER FOR MELTING WAX

SMALL PAN FOR MELTING STEARIC ACID

·   AND LUSTER CRYSTALS

SPOON FOR STIRRING, IF NEEDED

VOTIVE MOLDS (an ice cube tray works well)

WIRE-CORE WICKS

WICK TABS

MOLD RELEASE SPRAY

WICK HOLDER (knitting needle, piece of wire)

SMALL LADLE FOR POURING WAX INTO MOLDS

- Prepare the molds by spraying them with mold release spray.
- Cut wicks to size, leaving an extra 2 inches to warp around wick holder.
- Insert wicks in wick tabs and place at bottom of each votive mold.
- Tie other end of wick to wick holder, making sure wick is taut when holder is placed on top edge of votive mold.
- Melt wax until it reaches 190° F
- Melt stearic acid and luster crystals separately and add them to paraffin.
- Add fragrance and dyes if desired.
- Ladle wax into molds, making sure not to overfill periodically. Poke holes in wax as it hardens to remove air pockets and refill with more melted wax if necessary.
- Allow wax to harden for one hour or until cool.
- Place in the refrigerator for 10 minutes to facilitate mold removal.

Sand Candle Recipe

Making a candle using sand as mold is so much fun that the next thing you know, your house will be filled with wicked sculptures made in sand. The process by which wax is poured into sand is called casting but it is similar to the pouring method, except here, sand is the mold.

Casting candles in sand allows for much flexibility and creative free-forming in terms of the shape of the candle. A footprint, a pyramid, a hand print can be defined in damp sand as easily as the shape made by placing a small bowl in sand and removing it, or a small box. Also, multiple wicks can be used, especially if the cast shape is large but flat. Imagine a hand print cast in sand, with one wick at each fingertip and two in the palm.

The temperature at which the wax is poured into the sand will determine whether or not the sand will stick to the outer surface of the candle, depending on the desired effect. If the temperature of the wax is 150° F to 165° F when poured, the sand will not stick to the outside of the candle when it is removed; on the other hand, if the wax is within the 245° F to 290° F range, the sand will stick to the outer layer of the candle for a sand-encrusted effect.

Ingredients

- PARAFFIN WAX WITH A HIGH MELTING POINT, AMOUNT WILL DEPEND ON SIZE OF MOLDED SHAPE
- DYES AND SCENTS, IF DESIRED

Equipment

- DOUBLE BOILER FOR MELTING WAX
- A SPOON OR FORK TO DISSIPATE THE STREAM OF MELTED WAX WHEN POURED
- CLEAN BEACH SAND, FREE OF DEBRIS
- WATER FOR WETTING SAND
- ONE LARGE BOX OR CONTAINER TO PLACE SAND IN
- WIRE-CORE WICK

- POURING PITCHER FOR POURING THE MELTED WAX INTO THE SAND
- THIN KNITTING NEEDLE OR SMALL SIZE DRILL BIT FOR MAKING HOLES IN THE CANDLE FOR WICKING

- *Place clean sand in box or container and add enough water to the sand so that it is moist, packed and holds its shape when something is placed in it and removed. Do not over water sand.*
- *Melt wax until it reaches either the 150° F to 160° F or the 245° F to 290° F range, depending on whether or not you are going for the sand-encrusted look.*
- *Add dyes and scents to melted wax if desired.*
- *Pour wax slowly into sand mold, using a spoon or fork to interrupt the stream of hot wax. If the stream is not interrupted or dissipated when it hits the sand, the sand will lose its shape.*
- *Slowly the wax will seep into the sand; keep pouring until the mold gradually fills up.*
- *Once the wax has stopped seeping through neighboring sand, gently poke holes in the wax to remove air bubbles and pockets and to ensure that all seepage has stopped; pour additional wax if need be to refill holes.*
- *If your molded shape is relatively shallow (2 inches and under), wait until the wax has just started to harden but is still soft enough that you can insert one (or more) wicks into the wax, leaving a bit sticking up at the top.*
- *Allow the candle to dry for 3 to 4 hours until it is completely hard.*
- *If your molded shape is deeper than two inches, allow the candle to dry for at least 4 hours or until it is completely hard, then remove the candle from the sand. Take a very thin knitting needle or a small size drill bit, warm it up by placing it boiling water for a few minutes. Take the warm needle or drill bit and pierce one or more holes into the wax. Thread wick through hole (or holes). If the hole drilled is too big, take a bit of melted wax and pour over the hole from both sides of the candle, sealing the wick into the candle.*

Basic Container Candle Recipe

This basic recipe can be adapted to most container candles, large or small. Select a wick according to the size of your container and type of wax used. Small size flat braid wicks for candles with a 2 inch diameter or less; medium flat-braid wicks for candles with a 2 to 5 inch diameter, and large size flat braid wicks for candles with a 5 inch diameter or more. Square braided wicks should be used for candles made from pure beeswax or beeswax–paraffin blends. If your container is deep (over 1½ to 2 inches), use a wick tab to keep the wick in place at the bottom of the container and a wick holder for attaching the wick. If your container is under 2 inches deep (a seashell, walnut shell, or eggshell), there is no need for a wick holder; simply use wire core wicks with wick tabs and the wick will stand on its own, provided the wax is carefully poured.

Ingredients

- PARAFFIN WAX WITH A LOW TO
  MEDIUM MELTING POINT
  *(the amount of wax can be estimated by using
  the method on page 60)*
- SCENTS AND DYES, IF DESIRED

Equipment

- DOUBLE BOILER FOR MELTING WAX
- 1 SMALL RAMEKINS OR CUSTARD CUPS
- SMALL SIZE WIRE-CORE WICK
- WICK TAB
- SMALL LADLE FOR POURING MELTED
  WAX INTO THE CUPS

- *Make sure that your containers are clean and dry.*
- *Cut a piece of wire-core wick long enough so that when placed in the cup, 1 inch of the wick sticks out from the top.*
- *Attach wick to wick tab and place at bottom of the container.*
- *Melt the wax until it reaches 185° F. to 190° F.*
- *Add dyes and scents if desired.*
- *Slowly ladle wax into the cup, filling it three-quarters of the way up.*
- *Make sure top end of wick is straight and not drowning in wax.*
- *Let cool for 3 to 4 hours or until wax is completely hard.*

BASIC MOLDED CANDLE RECIPES

A molded candle can be as simple and elegant as a traditional pillar, or as complex and intricately detailed as a replica of a Ming Dynasty figurine. It can be a freeform wicked mass pulled from a shaped nest of aluminum foil or a square beam from an empty milk carton. Regardless of the mold—commercial, traditional, disposable or not—the process remains the same: pouring melted wax into a shape that holds the wax until it hardens, after which the mold is removed.

The only other variances, other than the type of mold used, is in the wax you use, (beeswax, paraffin, beeswax–paraffin blend), the temperature at which the wax should be poured (disposable, improvised molds tend to withstand lower temperatures than the commercial kind) the size of the wick and additives selected.

The recipe below is incredibly simple and requires minimal time and equipment. It's a good place for the novice candlemaker to start.

Lavender Mini Pillar

Ingredients

- 1 POUND PARAFFIN WAX WITH MEDIUM MELTING POINT (130°F TO 145°F)
- 1/4 POUND PARAFFIN WAX WITH A HIGH MELTING POINT (OVER 145°F)
- 6 DROPS LAVENDER ESSENTIAL OIL
- 1 PURPLE CRAYON, PAPER REMOVED, CUT IN PIECES
- 1/2 CUP CRUSHED LAVENDER FLOWERS

Equipment

- DOUBLE BOILER FOR MELTING WAX
- SPOON FOR STIRRING, IF NEEDED
- EMPTY SOUP CAN

equipment continued . . .

- • MOLD RELEASE OR SILICONE SPRAY
- • 30 OR 32-PLY FLAT-BRAIDED WICK
- • WICK HOLDER *(pencil, chopstick or knitting needle)*
- • WICK WEIGHT *(washer or small bolt)*
- • BAKING SHEET
- • SMALL PAINTBRUSH
- • SKILLET OR PAN FOR EVENING OUT
  BOTTOM OF CANDLE *(optional)*
- • LADLE

- Prepare soup can (mold) by spraying the inside with mold release or silicone spray.
- Spread out lavender flowers on baking sheet and set aside.
- Cut a piece of wick that is at least 2 inches longer than the height of the can.
- Attach the weight on one end of the wick and place at bottom of can.
- Attach the other end to the wick holder, making it taut enough so that there is no slack when the wick holder is resting on the top edges of the soup can.
- Melt medium melting point paraffin wax in double boiler until it reaches between 185° F and 190° F.
- Add crayon pieces to melted wax and stir until fully dissolved.
- Add lavender essential oil.
- Ladle wax into soup can until can is filled.
- Alow wax to harden and cool (about 3 hours).
- Remove candle from mold.
- Even out bottom of candle by placing it on a hot skillet or griddle and melting for a few seconds.
- Melt high melting point paraffin wax in double boiler until it reaches 200° F to 210° F.
- With the small paintbrush, cover the exterior of the candle with wax and roll it into the baking sheet containing lavender flowers.

Rolled candles—pillars or tapers—are elegant in their simplicity and appeal. They also happen to be the easiest candles to make, as they require the least amount of effort, tools, equipment and ingredients.

All you need to make a rolled candle is sheet wax and a wick.

There are three different types of sheet waxes, ranging from most to least expensive: pure unadulterated honeycomb sheet wax (beeswax), honeycomb–paraffin blended sheets or paraffin sheets. Sheets are usually 8 inches by 16 inches, and can be sliced in half lengthwise with a sharp knife to make shorter pillars or tapers. The sheets must be at room temperature in order to roll without cracking or breaking. Sheets can be warmed before rolling with a blow dryer if necessary. But be careful, wax sheets are thin and can melt very easily.

With beeswax sheets, use a medium flat-braided 30–or 32-ply wick. For paraffin sheets or paraffin–beeswax blended sheets, a number 5 (medium) square-braided wick is ideal. Cut the wick so that it is two inches longer than the length of the candle you want to make. Place the sheet wax on a flat surface and position the wick along the short edge of the sheet in such a way that the wick is parallel to the edge and that there is about one inch of wick sticking out at either end of the sheet. Fold over a little bit of the wax and press firmly on the wick, sealing it in place. Slowly roll the wax, applying firm pressure to avoid trapping air bubbles between rolls. Make sure that you are rolling in a straight line so that edges of the candle will be even on both sides. After the sheet is completely rolled, trim the bottom of the candle flat with a sharp knife. Heat a skillet or pan and place the bottom of the candle on the hot surface so as to gently melt it. This process will also melt the rolls together, preventing any chance that they might loosen or unroll.

PROBLEM	CAUSE	SOLUTION
Air bubbles in wax:	wax poured too cold	• gently scrape them off, if they're at the surface; next time, pour at hotter temperature
	poured too fast	• pour more slowly
Air trapped when pouring:		• gently tap mold when pouring to release air
	candle cooled in draft	• keep out of drafts when cooling
Candle stuck in mold:	poured too hot	• put candle in freezer for a few minutes; it may pop out
	not enough mold release	• use more mold release or silicone spray next time
	stearic acid was used	• don't use stearic acid with rubber or plastic molds
Cracks in candle:	cooled to fast	• check the temperature of cool water bath to make sure it's not too cold
Mottled exterior:	cooled too fast	• check temperature of water bath
Too much oil in wax:		• use harder wax
	too much mold release	• use less
Wrong type of fragrance:		• fragrance must be the type that mixes with wax; try using less fragrance
"Frost" marks on surface:	poured too cold	• increase pouring temp.
	mold too cold	• warm mold before pouring
	too much stearic acid	• use less

PROBLEM	CAUSE	SOLUTION
Lines/seams on surface:		
	lines/seams in mold	• *polish surface with a nylon stocking*
Candle chips easily:	too much stearic acid	• *use less*
Flame Sputters:	water in wick or wax	• *make sure wick is dry*
		• *prime wick*
		• *make sure no water in wax*
Flame smokes:	high oil content of wax	• *use harder wax*
	wick is too large	• *use smaller wick*
Air pockets in candle:		• *pour at higher temperature and tap candle when pouring to release trapped air*
Wick too long:		• *trim wick regularly*
Candle burns unevenly:	candle in draft	• *keep out of drafts*
Flame drowns in melted wax pool:		
	wick too small	• *use large size wick*
	wax too soft	• *use harder wax or add more stearic acid*
	wick is clogged	• *use less dyes and/or scents*
Flame too small:	wick too small	• *use larger wick*
	wax too hard	• *change to wax with a lower melting point*
Wick only burns out center of candle instead of fuller diameter:		
	wax too hard	• *use softer wax*
	wick too small	• *use larger wick*

CANDLE MAKING SAFETY TIPS

- Never pour melted wax down the drain; it will harden and clog your pipes.

- Always make sure there is enough water in the bottom part of your double boiler.

- Cover your work area with newspaper in case of wax spills.

- Never leave melting wax unattended.

- If your melting wax ignites, cover it with a lid and turn off the heat source.

- Keep a can of baking soda or a damp rag on hand to extinguish wax fires.

- Do not put out burning wax with water; this will just cause the flames to scatter.

- If you get hot melted wax on your finger, submerge it immediately in cold water and carefully peel off the wax when cool.

Part ii

Making Potpourri

Perfumes, incenses and potpourri—be they for mood-setting, olfactory pleasures, religious rites or even odor concealing—have held a prominent place in our history since biblical times.

Biblical passages (Exodus 30:23 and 30:34) tell of holy oil created with myrrh, frankincense, cinnamon, calamus and cassia. The early Egyptians use of scent is well-documented. Aromatic plants were burned in the home, floors were scattered with sweet-smelling leaves, and the dead were buried with their favorite perfumes beside them. The highest Egyptian priests were famous for their signature scents, and despite their arduous efforts to keep their recipes secret, were the inspiration for common use of scent. In fact, many of the most commonly used ingredients of Cleopatra's time are still being used widely today, including cinnamon, juniper, frankincense and myrrh. Of course, possibly her most famous use of scent and flowers was the seductive carpeting of rose petals (rumored to be over a foot deep) that no doubt worked wonders for Mark Anthony as he made his way to her boudoir.

Early Greek and Roman civilizations were also renowned for their use of scent, going so far as to scent not only their bodies and their homes but their domestic animals as well.

With the development of international trade, the exotic herbs, spices and flowers of far-away lands like Egypt became much sought after commodities. Trade and travel coincided with the explosive development of civilized living in urban areas in European countries, with which came the obvious noxious results — overcrowding, little personal hygiene and public sanitation, scarce fresh water and few means to disguise the overpowering odors of daily life.

Potpourri, perfumes, unguents and incense became a necessary part of life. In 16th century England, during the reign of Elizabeth I, the use of herbs to freshen the stagnant odors of the home was de rigeur. Floors were covered with herbs specially chosen to freshen each room at a footstep, and the forerunners to today's potpourri— floral and herbal mixtures in bags—were used to sweeten closets, freshen the air and to deter vermin.

Other creative uses for scented botanicals existed, too. Pillows and mattresses were stuffed with rose petals. Hops were even added for both their soporific effect and their softness. People carried personal bouquets, called nosegays, with them to sweeten the air around them. Sachets were strategically placed throughout the home. During the Victorian Era (1837–1901), ladies became experts at creating

their own signature scents in the form of pot pourri, most often using the carefully cultivated ingredients from their own gardens, including flowers, herbs, spices and pine cones. The Victorians studied plants and flowers assiduously – every item was believed to have specific properties, and consequently, specific uses.

Early potpourris were moist blends (potpourri literally means 'rotten pot' or 'rot pot' in French) created from fresh flower petals (usually roses), salt and herbs that were aged in a sealed glass container. While a much more intense aroma is the result of this method, the visual results are not as pleasing. Moist potpourri does actually look quite rotten, as the vibrant color of the petals fades away to brown. On the other hand, moist mixtures last much longer, as does their aroma.

Today, aromatherapy is a thriving area of study. Many believe that our olfactory sense triggers important emotional cues, and that scent and aroma can be used effectively to alter or enhance mood. We all have experienced the evocative sensation that the aroma of fresh-baked bread or apple pie brings on, or the unexplained emotions that flood us when a scent reminiscent of our childhood is evident. Potpourri can be a subtle addition to the environment of your home, and help you to think of spring warmth or fall efficiencies, help to relax or to stimulate, and to create a sensual atmosphere throughout.

Potpourri can be made with virtually any organic—and sometimes synthetic—materials. The basic elements are: Filler (dried flower petals, buds, fruit, mosses, bark, sequins, beads, etc.); Fragrance (fragrant oils, essential oils, particularly aromatic dried flowers, herbs and fruits); and Fixatives (spices, mosses, roots and powders that preserve the fragrance in a potpourri mixture).

The steps to making a fragrant, attractive potpourri begin in the garden (or the florist)—or you can buy dried flowers (see page 170 for a list of suppliers), skip the first few steps and compose from there. Essentially, the steps to making potpourri are these:

1. Collect your ingredients—take notes! It's always nice to know where you started & what ingredients you chose.

2. Dry the elements.

3. Combine the dried ingredients.

4. Mix the fragrance and the fixatives.

5. Add fragrance–fixative mixture to dried elements.

6. Age the potpourri in a sealed container in a dark dry place, mixing every day or so.

7. Pick out decorative containers, display your potpourri and infuse your home with wonderful scents!

With the exception of a few ingredients, in particular synthetic fixatives, most of the tools you will need for creating aromatic potpourri blends can be gathered in your kitchen, garage or attic.

- GARDEN CLIPPERS: for gathering your own botanicals. Use a sharp pair for a clean cut.

- PRUNING SHEARS: Helpful if you intend to gather anything with thick or tough stems.

- COLLECTING BASKET: to hold your freshly cut flowers, branches, pine cones or herbs.

- AIRTIGHT BOX or TIN: for drying botanicals with a desiccant

- GLASS JARS (with lids or plastic container with air-tight lid): to store your mixtures while they are aging

- RUBBER BANDS: for drying bunches of flowers and herbs. Sometimes rubber bands work better than string, as stems can change shape and size when drying.

- STRING: for hanging bunches of botanicals while they dry

- SAND: fine, pure sand can be used as a drying agent for many flowers. You can purchase what is called "silver sand" at most hardware stores, home or garden supply stores and craft stores.

- SMALL PAINTBRUSH: to apply silica to delicate flowers

- SPRAY BOTTLE (optional): for evenly spraying liquid fixatives on potpourri

- FOOD DEHYDRATOR (optional): for drying flowers, fruits, leaves, vegetables. Available at most good kitchen stores.

- COFFEE GRINDER, SPICE MILL or BLENDER (optional): for grinding herbs, spices, and orris root (fixative)

- FLAT BASKET or SCREEN: for drying leaves, citrus and other materials.

- STAINLESS STEEL MEASURING SPOONS: to measure fixatives.

- GLASS or STAINLESS STEEL MEASURING CUPS: to measure bulk ingredients.

- LARGE CERAMIC MIXING BOWL: for blending filler, fragrance and fixative.

- MIXING SPOON: to thoroughly blend ingredients

- PESTLE AND MORTAR: for crushing herbs and spices.

- GLASS DROPPER: for measuring essential or fragrance oils.

- SILICA GEL: for drying botanicals; available from most florists or hobby shops.

- NOTEPAD AND PENCIL: to keep track of ingredients or to record your own creations

Potpourri consists of three basic elements
FILLER, FRAGRANCE & FIXATIVE

Filler

"Filler" is the body of the potpourri: a variety of botanical elements—including colorful flowers, leaves, herbs, fruits, berries, nuts, woods, barks, mosses and pinecones—that make potpourri a visual and aromatic addition to every home. Each element of the body plays a specific role in the final recipe through its distinct size, shape, color and texture (see Filler Properties, below).

In addition to providing the aesthetic canvas for creating customized fragrant blends through the use of oils and essences, these botanicals also lend their own subtle fragrance to potpourri, particularly scented flower petals.

Traditionally, potpourri featured roses as the main floral ingredient, but today's creative mixtures draw on almost every flower imaginable from the sturdy roadside flower to the exotic bloom. There are endless flowers to choose from, ranging from azalea petals to zinnias, each with its own set of characteristics and properties. Petals, buds or entire dried flowers are used.

Among the most popular floral ingredients are baby's breath, globe amaranth, calendula, delphinium, carnations, larkspur, marigolds, and lavender. Many of these flowers are available already dried through bulk potpourri suppliers (a listing of key sources appears at the end of the book). However, one derives a certain satisfaction from harvesting and drying your own potpourri ingredients (see Drying Methods page 112).

FLOWERS			
NAME	**COLOR(S)**	**PROPERTIES/DESCRIPTION**	**DRYING METHOD**
BABY'S BREATH *Gypsophila paniculata*	white	tiny white flowers delicate, often available dry use entire stem or flowers signified everlasting love during Victorian times	air
CARNATION *Dianthus caryophyllus*	red	indicated bonds of affection traditionally	air/silica
DAISIES *Chrysanthemum Leucanthemum*	white	Victorian symbol of simplicity	air
FOX GLOVE *Digitalis purpurea*	purple, lavender, to white	beautiful and interesting finger-shaped blooms on long stem	air/desiccant, air, use entire stalk or flowers
FREESIA *Freesia refraca*	mostly yellows, some purples, pinks, reds	stems of elegant tubular flowers	desiccant
GERANIUM *Pelargonium zonale*	red, white, pink	use the pelargonium species for a wonderful scent. symbol of gentility (Victorian times)	air use individual petals Or the entire flower
GLOBE *Amaranth*	red, pink, orange, white	rich color, longlasting flower, retains fragrance well Victorians believed flower symbolized unfailing affection.	air
GLOBE THISTLE *Echinops ritro*	blue	use before flower develops bold architectural shape	

FLOWERS (continued)			
NAME	**COLOR(S)**	**PROPERTIES/DESCRIPTION**	**DRYING METHOD**
HYDRANGEA *arborescens*	white	*beautiful and versatile flower*	air/press
HYDRANGEA *macrophylla*	blue, pink	*classic, romantic style and color*	use either entire flower or florets
JASMINE *various species*	white	*oriental aroma/exotic bloom, indicated amiability traditionally*	desiccant
LAVENDER *Lavandula angustifolium*	purples/blues	*Clean crisp scent. Long lasting, Use entire stem or crumbled flowers. Widely commercially available. Victorians used it to symbolize devotion and cleanliness*	air
LARKSPUR *delphinium ambigua*	pink, blue, white	*Easily air-dried. Bright lasting color. Use full stalk*	air
LARKSPUR *Delphinium elatum*	blue, lilac, pink, white	*symbol of lightness and levity*	air
MARIGOLD *Tagetes patula*	bright oranges, yellows	*strong lasting colors, fragile when dry*	air/oven
MIMOSA *Acacia dealbata*	yellow	*striking exotic, use entire branch or ind'l flower*	air/press
ORCHID	white, pink	*exotic, highly fragrant. Great to use whole flower as topnote decoration*	desiccant
PEONY *Paeonia lactiflora*	pink, red, white, cream	*lavish blooms, Victorian – symbolized Shyness.*	air Use bud /flower

FLOWERS *(continued)*			
ROSES	red, pink, orange, cream	*classic potpourri ingredient, use petals, buds, leaves, or flowers, symbolizes luxury/ romance/love widely, available dried*	air or yellow, desiccant
STATICE	blue, purple, pink, white, yellow	*fragile when dry, widely available, use full stem/cluster of blooms*	desiccant
STRAWFLOWER *Hilichrysum bracteatum*	red, pink, orange, yellow	*sturdy flower with bright colors perfect for many recipes. Whole flower or petals. Victorian symbol of friendship*	air/desiccant
SUNFLOWERS *Helianthus annuus*	bright yellows	*excellent color retention, petals or whole flower*	air
TULIP	red, yellow, white, pink/purple	*a striking addition to any mix. Use the entire flowerhead for drama*	desiccant
YARROW *Achillea millefolium*	pink	*air dries well, flat-headed flower. Use the petals or the entire flower. Vict. Symbol of health Yarrow, milfoil yellow*	air
ZINNIA *Zinnia elegans*	yellow, orange, red	*the rich tones of this flower are perfect for Fall arrangements. Very Hardy, and easy to find. Use the entire dried flowerhead Victorian reminder of friendship.*	desiccant

Dried fruits and berries are a great resource for their texture, shape and fragrance and certainly for their color. Lemons, limes, oranges and kumquats dry easily and look great, either as whole fruit, slices, or peels. Dried grapefruit and pomegranate slices can be used for dramatic visual effect, and dried apple slices or skins make for a fragrant addition. Berries—vibrant bursts of color— are particularly easy to work with as there is no slicing or peeling involved. Cranberries, blueberries, rose hips and even peppercorns balance out with both their shape and scent longer, leafier elements such as eucalyptus leaves, lemongrass and holly. Remember to add more exotic elements as well, such as dried banana slices and pineapple slices.

FRUITS, VEGETABLES & BERRIES

NAME/TYPE	DESCRIPTION AND USES
APPLES	*delightful in aroma and easy to prepare, dried apple slices add a homey and warm scent to fall mixes*
ARTICHOKES	*baby artichokes are a particularly interesting additions to potpourri, keep them whole for a dramatic contrasting element*
BERRIES	*use them whole*
ALLSPICE	*these brown berries lend a spicy fragrance to mix*
BLUEBERRIES	*seasonal*
CRANBERRIES	*seasonal*
JUNIPER	*crushed or whole, these berries lend a woodsy appeal and aroma*
CITRUS	*almost any citrus fruit can be used in multiple ways peel off the skin of whole dried fruits, or chunks of*
GRAPEFRUITS LEMONS LIMES KUMQUATS ORANGES	*peel add both fragrance and visual interest*
CORN	*dried kernels of indian corn are colorful and seasonal in fall recipes*
POMEGRANATES	*easy to dry at home (scoop out the seeds from one end, and dry in oven), this fruit lends an exotic air to your potpourri*
PEACHES	*romantic and sweet, dried peach slices are well utilized in feminine mixes of peach and pink petal base.*

Herbs such as dill, chamomile, coriander, hops, marjoram, rosemary and oregano are just a sampling of the commonly found herbs often included in potpourris blends. Spices include cloves, cardamom, root ginger, cinnamon, nutmeg, vanilla and star anise. True potpourri aficionados grind their own spices in a coffee grinder, blender or with a mortar and pestle. The aroma is certainly more powerful than that of pre-crushed, or store-bought varieties.

HERBS & SPICES		
NAME	**DESCRIPTION**	**USE**
BASIL *Ocimum basilicum*	*pretty, medium-sized leaves.* *with aromatic smell.* *In Victorian times, its' use* *implied "best wishes or love"*	leaves
BERGAMOT *Monarda didyma*	*pretty red flowers*	flowers and leaves
CARDAMOM SEED		*these seeds lend an earthy* *exotic scent seeds and* *work well in citrus or* *oriental mixes*
CHAMOMILE	*little yellow flowers*	

HERBS & SPICES *(continued)*		
NAME	**DESCRIPTION**	**USE**
CHAMOMILE *Chamaemelum* *nubile*	*little yellow flowers*	flowers and leaves
CINNAMON	*wonderful aromatic aroma,* *bark/whole sticks of interesting* *and dramatic linear shape,* *associated with holidays*	small pieces
CLOVE *Eugenia* *caryophyllata*	*strongly scented unopened flower* *bud, wonderful shape and aroma,* *associated with holidays*	whole or crushed
CORIANDER *Coriandrum* *sativum*	*with a spicy overtone*	seeds, crushed or whole
DILL *Anethum* *graveolens*	*fresh herbal scent flowers and/or* *leaves*	little yellow flowers
HOPS *Humulus lupulus*	*light green herb known for* *soporific affect*	flowers and or leaves
LEMON BALM *Melissa officinalis*	*lovely citrus aroma*	leaves
LEMON VERBENA *Aloysia triphylla*	*leaves have a wonderful and* *distinct lemony aroma*	leaves
MARJORAM/OREGANO *Origanum* *majorana*	*rust-colored fragrant herb with* *flowers and or leaves*	clusters of tiny pink florets
MINT *Mentha*	*small flowers gather around a stem* *leaves or stem, clean fresh scent*	

Marigold

Marjoram

HERBS & SPICES *(continued)*

NAME	DESCRIPTION	USE
NUTMEG *Myristica fragrans*	tree seed with strong aromatic aroma	whole nut or grated kernel
PATCHOULI *Pogostemon cablin*	aromatic herb often used in oriental mixes	leaves
ROSEMARY *Rosmarinus Officinalis*	long, pine-needle like leaves, lend a wonderful herbal smell	leaves, stems and flowers
SAGE *Salvia officinalis*	purple and pink flowers	leaves
STAR ANISE	little star-shaped form with a pretty and slightly sweet scent, perfect for spicy or citrus blends	seed
SWEET BAY *Laurus Nobilis*	pretty leaves make this herb perfect for kitchen blends, also known as laurel or bayleaf	leaves
THYME Thymus	pink	flowers and or leaves
VANILLA pods/bean *vanilla planifola*	fragrant and exotic warm and sensual aroma	whole or crushed pod

Leaves, Wood, Moss, Cones, Nuts, Seeds, Grasses & Resins

Alongside vibrant flowers are leaves, many of which add not only a pleasing background for your palette, but also their own distinct aroma. Almost any leaf can be used. There are large, lacy looks such as fern, small rounded leaves like boxwood, colorful maple leaves collected during fall wood strolls, and the flat translucent honesty leaf. Leaves of herbs lend another component to your blend – try mint, basil, thyme, rosemary, lavender or lemon verbena. Other botanicals, including barks, pine cones, mosses, nuts and even seeds, round out most recipes, and can lend interesting visual elements. Easy to find, and pertinent to winter potpourri mixes, are the cones of birch, cedar, hemlock or pine trees. Some of these have fixative qualities as well, helping to prolong the life of the mix.

Wood—curled or chipped—add elegance and depth to most blends. Try hickory or cedar curls (easily found in pet stores), or sassafras and sandalwood; all lend wonderful subtle fragrance. Apple wood can be a great addition to spring mixes. Chunks of bark lend an earthy backdrop, and can range from whites to greens and browns. Gather your bark from the trails along your fall wood walks, but remember to never peel bark from a live tree! Sheet moss is inexpensive, readily available (any well-stocked floral supply store or craft source should carry it), acts as a secondary fixative and looks wonderful in almost any recipe.

* (see also spice chart)

LEAVES, WOODS, MOSS, CONES, NUTS, SEEDS, GRASSES & RESINS		
TYPE BARK	NAMES	DESCRIPTION • *almost any bark can be used; try chunks, curls, strips, or make your own shapes. Bark also has a fixative quality, working well to absorb fragrance.*
	BIRCHBARK	• *the white birch offers pretty curls.*

LEAVES, WOODS, MOSS, CONES, NUTS, SEEDS, GRASSES & RESINS		
BARK	CINNAMON*	• aromatic
	SASSAFRAS	• woodsy and aromatic
	CONES- small (hemlock, larch, birch)	• use small cones whole. • apply your essential oils directly to the cones. They act as a fixative as well as being decorative
EVERGREEN NEEDLES AND TIPS	CONES – large (pine, cedar, spruce, fir)	• large cones can be used whole as decorative accents, or broken down into parts, or individual scales • use the fragrant bits from the pine, hemlock, or any evergreen for a great design element in winter potpourris
FERNS		• lacy, intricate, architectural, long or lean, ferns are a versatile potpourri ingredient
GUM RESINS	FRANKINCENSE	• the hardened resin from the bark of the boswellia thurifera tree, a staple of Biblical and Egyptian perfumery. Frankincense is also a secondary fixative.
	MYRRH	• a gum resin with an oriental aroma that has biblical roots much like frankincense. Myrrh also has fixative properties.
GRASSES	VETIVER	• this tall elegant grass is both a beautiful and fragrant potpourri ingredient. It has a slightly aromatic, earthy fragrance, perfect for woodsy mixes. Its essential oil has been a classic perfume ingredient for centuries.

LEAVES, WOODS, MOSS, CONES, NUTS, SEEDS, GRASSES & RESINS		
LEAVES	BEECH	• Small, pretty and sturdy leaves.
	BOXWOOD	• Dark and pretty.
	EUCALYPTUS	• Exquisite sprays of silvery leaves.
	HOLLY	• Air-dries exceptionally well these dry to a rich tone, and while gathered in the summer, when the tree has berries, remind us of the holidays. classically shaped, and abundant in many areas
	IVY	• Classically shaped, and abundant in many areas
	MAPLE	• Vibrantly colored fall maple leaves lend the perfect seasonal backdrop to fall mixes. Colors range from green to red to gold.
	ROSE	• With a delicate rose fragrance, and a sturdy makeup, rose leaves are a classic.
	UVA URSI	• Miniature green oval-shaped leaves that are a charming and versatile potpourri ingredient. They have no scent.
	WOODRUFF	• Little oblong leaves with a lasting hay-like aroma.
LICHEN	OAK MOSS	• Oak moss is a widely used lichen. Oak moss has a gray and delicate appearance that is a good backdrop for potpourri. Oak moss is a very effective fixative.

LEAVES, WOODS, MOSS, CONES, NUTS, SEEDS, GRASSES & RESINS		
MOSS	Sheet moss	• Moss is often used as a potpourri ingredient, as it brings both a fixative quality and a pretty design influence. This moss is widely commercially available.
MUSHROOMS	Sponge mushrooms	• These mushrooms feature one grooved side and one smooth. They are readily available from commercial potpourri suppliers and lend an interesting visual effect to woodsy or holiday mixes.
NUTS		• Almost any dried nut can be used for potpourri. Acorns and hickory are two of the most widely used varieties. You can use nuts whole, or even use interesting bits of shells to add to your recipes.
ROOTS	GINGER ROOT	• Dried chunks of ginger root add a fragrant and interesting touch to oriental/spicy mixtures.
SEEDHEADS/PODS	HONESTY	• Also called money plant, or silverdollar, these shimmery, almost transparent seedpods are unique. Their delicate look makes them a wonderful backdrop for floral arrangements.
	LOTUS SEEDHEADS	• Lunar looking lotus seedheads can be purchased through most bulk suppliers. Round with holes throughout, they add a unique look.
SEEDS		• The seeds of herbs are particularly popular with potpourri makes due to their fragrant nature.

What gives a filler its particular set of properties and distinctive role in the potpourri blend are its color, shape, size, scent and fragrance, and texture.

Color

When customizing potpourri blends, color can play a critical part in the design scheme. Whether creating a gift for a friend's newly renovated room in particular shades of blue, or a unique mix in a special corner of your home, combining and playing with colors in potpourri blends adds a personalized touch. Think also of color as a visual reminder of seasons or holidays. The reds and greens of Christmas, oranges, browns and yellows of fall or Thanksgiving, the exuberantly bright reds, yellows, greens and whites at Easter, and vibrant yellows and deep purples of summer flowers. We take emotional cues from color too—reds make us feel romantic, greens earthy, yellow gives a sense of well being. As a basic principle, colors that are close to each other on the spectrum will blend well together. Think of reds, yellows and oranges, or blues and violets. The farther apart the colors, the more dramatic a look that will occur. For example, yellow and purple, or red and blue blossoms, make for a very intense look. Green is an effective equilibrating background color, helping to blend and soften your floral tones.

Shape and Size

Nature has given us endless floral forms to work with. Think of a palette of shape, as you would of color, when working with dried materials. Flowers come in a wide variety of shapes. Among the 'ball' shaped blooms are roses, peonies and carnations. Foxglove, delphinium, gladiolas and hyacinth are all columnar in shape. Daisies, asters, sunflowers and strawflowers share a shape, as do the "cup"shaped peony, camellia and anemone. Not to be overlooked are flowers with sculptural shapes, such as tulips, orchids, and iris.

Added to the wide palette of floral shapes are the long and lean grasses, architectural pine cones, rounded berries or fruits. Fiddlehead ferns add a unique spiral element. You can experiment with your own shapes, too. Citrus peel can be carved to create interesting new forms, pine cone petals pinched and leaves sliced diagonally.

Often the most interesting potpourris contain surprising juxtapositions of shape and size. Use several larger elements, such as a whole fruit or stick or pinecone, to add an interesting dimension. Reserve the best preserved specimens of large flowers to place on top of your mixture.

Texture

Contrasting textures add an important element to potpourri. Spiny thistles mixed with soft petals, rough bark bits next to rounded citrus slices make for a more original visual feast.

Scent and Fragrance

While the main part played by your filler, or botanicals, is their visual aspects, botanic elements in blends add their own unique scent. Most flowers lose their scent during the drying process, but the wonderful fragrance of roses and lavender tends to linger on longer than most. Spices and herbs, whether whole or powdered, also make powerful fragrance enhancers.

Alongside the subtle aromas of the filler ingredients are the intense scents provided by essential oils (actually distilled directly from plants) or fragrance or perfume oils (laboratory-created fragrances made to evoke nature's aromas). These scents generally fall into one of four basic categories: spicy or animal (think of musks, patchouli, nutmeg), floral, fruity or citrus, and mint or herbal scents.

Essential oils are directly extracted from a flower or plant, through a process called steam distillation. In addition to their powerful aroma, essential oils have many therapeutic qualities, some relieving stress and fatigue, others providing invigorating effect or soothing properties. The most popular essential oils used for potpourri include geranium, lavender, lily-of-the-valley, lemon verbena, gardenia, eucalyptus, rose and citronella.

Laboratory-made fragrance or perfume oils generally are a combination of aromatic notes selected to work in harmony. While synthetic fragrances tend to simulate aromas found in nature, the fragrance industry has developed an array of scents that evoke a feeling, rather than a smell: freshly washed linen, ocean breeze or clean mountain air. These particular aromas blend well with summer or spring potpourris.

When choosing your fragrance, test several brands and types. Scent is personal and store-bought oils can vary in aroma and strength. Remember also that with fragrance oils and aromas, a little goes a very long way as they are highly concentrated: Use small quantities at first in creating your own recipes and test the strength of your ingredients. Choosing an oil close in fragrance to your filler is a good first step for those experimenting with aroma. Once you have learned your taste and tolerance level, you can experiment with multiple layers of fragrance, or more complicated perfume oils. Fragrant flowers and leaves add their signature scents, too, as do herbs and spices. As a guideline, use just under 15 drops of essential oil mixed with one tablespoon of orris root for every cup of filler in the recipe. Mixing these two elements together ensures an even spreading of them among your mix. Remember when working with essential oils to always keep bottles out of the reach of children and not to apply them directly to your skin.

FIXATIVES

Fixatives help maintain the strength and preserve—or fix—the scent of fragrant oils in the potpourri. They are available in liquid, powdered or dried form. Among the most common of the fixatives is orrisroot, (available in powdered form, granules or chunks) and oakmoss, both readily found through potpourri suppliers. Orrisroot is extracted from the roots of the Florentine Iris. Approximately one tablespoon of orrisroot will fix the fragrance for one cup of dried materials.

NOTE: *In addition to its fixative qualities, orrisroot can lend a dusty look to potpourri blends, and may cause allergic reactions to individuals who are prone to them, making cellulose granules, below, more attractive.*

Less likely to cause an allergic reaction is another natural fixative, cellulose granules, derived from ground corncobs. Using slightly more fragrance oil when using this fixative is recommended, as the granules are very absorbent. Cellulose granules are inexpensive and are readily available at pet food stores—it is used as a litter for small mammals!

Oakmoss is a lichen—a moss-like plant—that is easily found through potpourri suppliers. Oakmoss has a silvery gray/green color and lacy appearance. It is an interesting ingredient, as it adds not only fixative qualities, but also makes an attractive backdrop for many mixes.

Other organic fixatives include vetiver, calamus root, ground gum benzoin (benjamin), patchouli, ambergris, and in certain recipes, the spices act as fixatives. The best results are achieved when the fixatives are finely powdered and distributed evenly throughout the mixture.

Drying
Methods &
Techniques

Air Drying

If you have gathered your own materials, begin the drying process soon after picking. Without doubt the simplest, least expensive and most common method is air-drying. It yields perfect results for most botanicals.

HANGING BUNCHES

This method is used primarily for drying botanicals with stems, such as flowers and herbs. Gather four to eight of the best looking flowers you can find, remove lower leaves and pat dry. Bind stems together with a rubber band, gently separating the flowers, pods and stems from one another with your fingers to ensure better drying of individual items. Attach a piece of string to the rubber band by which to hang the flowers or herbs. On hangers, clothes lines or a drying rack, hang bunches upside down so that they don't touch each other, and place them in a warm, dry, dark spot, preferably one with good air circulation. The ideal temperature for drying flowers and herbs is between 85°–120° F. In these conditions, most materials will dry within four to ten days. If your room is damp, you risk rotting your plants before they have a chance to dry; a space not sufficiently dark will hasten fading of blooms. An attic, garage or cupboard is ideal. Flowers are ready when the petals and stems are crisp. Keep in mind that large bunches will inhibit the inside stems from drying. Also, keep your bunches to one type of botanical; different things will dry at different speeds. As the bunches dry, they also add a decorative and fragrant touch to your home, barn or drying room.

(Note: Air drying may not be the ideal method for large blooms whose shape is the key element you are seeking, as this method will weaken their form. For these flowers, such as tulips, try desiccant drying as an alternative.)

FLAT METHODS

For flower heads, petals or leaves, or any item too small to tie in a bunch and hang-dry, flat drying is a perfect method. You will need a screen, a flat basket, or a shelf made of chicken wire-type material. Layer botanicals in a single layer so that they do not touch each other —this speeds the drying process. Choose a place that is dark, free from drafts, and between 85° F and 110° F. Flower heads, petals and leaves can dry in just 2 to 3 days. Depending on temperature and botanical, though, some items will take up to one week. To best preserve them, store in glass or plastic airtight containers. As an added measure, add one tablespoon of silica gel at the base of the container (for added protection against moisture.)

Evergreens should be treated slightly differently. Spread the fresh pieces (ideally 6 – 8" tips) in a flat basket or on screens or newspaper in a warm place. They dry best at temperatures between 70° F and 120° F. Try to keep the evergreens whole until you create your potpourri. Fruits and vegetables are well suited to air-drying. You can use entire small citrus fruits, such as lemons, key limes, small oranges, which dry well whole, or create swirls, chunks, thin slices or strips from the skin of your chosen fruit. To dry the peel, scoop all of the flesh or fruit from the skin, and cut the skin into the desired shape. Spread the pieces on a flat basket, taking care that there is only one layer. Leave the basket in a dry place with a temperature of about between 70° F – 100° F. This method will work for thin slices as well. Most fruits will dry completely within 3 days.

Pressing

This simple method of drying is almost universally applicable, easy and inexpensive. Keep in mind that the one drawback to pressing, however, comes with the form of the outcome: a two-dimensional form. Perhaps pick flowers to press that will be added as a top decorative note to your mixture when displayed.

As a general rule, flowers that are flat in shape to start with (such as pansies, violets, or small daisies) will yield better pressing results remaining truer to their original form. Leaves are well suited to pressing, as their form is already flat. As with all methods of drying, make sure to begin your pressing process soon after materials have been gathered. A formal "flower press" available in craft supply stores is ideal; however, a simple method using elements found in most homes works just as well. An outdated telephone directory, for example, provides both the weight and the absorbency of paper required.

Press flower heads, stems and leaves separately, with each page carrying one type of item. Items on a page should not touch one another. Start from the back of the book, placing your botanicals about every 40 pages. You can label the pages as you go, with tape tabs, post its or colored stickers.

When you have everything placed, place the directory in a warm dry spot and lay additional books on top. Most flowers will dry within 2 to 3 weeks.

Dehydrator Drying

A basic store-bought food dehydrator will quicken the drying process. Dehydrators work particularly well for fruit and vegetable slices, of course, but can also yield good results for flowers. Generally, the appliance will come with guidelines for drying slices of fruits and vegetables, and the time and temperatures vary from one unit to the next.

For flowers, try the following: layer the flower heads on the trays, always leaving space between them and always face up. Dry for 1 hour, then test. If not completely dry (crispy), return to the dehydrator and keep checking every quarter of an hour. When completely dry, let them cool on the trays before moving them.

Because the Dehydrator Method yields quick results, experiment freely with less traditional ingredients: cucumber and mango slices, whole miniature pomegranates and artichoke flowers.

Desiccant Drying

Desiccant drying using desiccants such as silica gel or sand can result in perfectly preserved and shaped botanicals, ideal for the top decorative touches to your mixture. This is a preferred method for large, elaborately shaped blooms, such as tulips, orchids, lilies and daffodils, whose shape you want to use as a key element in your potpourri.

SILICA GEL CRYSTALS

This is without doubt the most popular and effective drying method used today. While slightly more expensive than air drying, this method is important because of the quality of the results. Silica gel crystals are widely available at crafts shops, floral suppliers and even drugstores. Try to purchase those that have a color key – deep blue crystals mean they are fully dry, pink indicates there is remaining moisture. If very chunky, the crystals can be ground in a standard food processor or coffee grinder to a smaller, more manageable size, closer to sugar or coffee grains. Remember to thoroughly clean your food processor if you use this technique. Note: Silica gel crystals may be used over and over again simply by drying them in the oven at low heat (about 150° F) for a few hours between use. Find a flat-bottomed air-tight plastic container (ideally less than 6" deep) and pour a layer of silica gel crystals about 1" thick to cover the bottom. Place the whole flower heads to be dried on the gel, face up, making sure they are not touching. Slowly, using a spoon, pour additional crystals over the flowers, trying to fill the crevices, and eventually cover the flower heads. A fine brush can be helpful to push the gel into place, too. Be gentle! Your application of the silica will effect the final shape of your materials. Cover the box and leave in a warm spot for 3 days. Open the box and gently remove one specimen with a teaspoon to see if it is dry. Petals should have a paper-like feeling, and the stem should be completely dry. Remember – dried flower heads are fragile and can be damaged with you hands. To protect your flowers, spray them with some matte varnish.

SAND

Used for centuries, sand drying is still a very effect and cost-efficient drying method, although this method takes a long time to completely dry your botanicals. It is important to use the cleanest and driest sand available. The best choice is silver sand, available at most garden centers, but clean, dry beach sand will work as well. Find a shallow cardboard box, and spread a 1" layer of sand on the bottom. Place your flowers on the sand (again, they shouldn't touch!). Carefully cover the flowers with sand until they are completely hidden. Place the uncovered box in a warm, dry place. Using sand to dry your plant material can take up to four weeks. Test the dryness at about one week, and then again the second week and so forth.

OVEN DRYING

A fast and easy method, oven-drying should be reserved for those materials whose color is not an integral element, and that will be crushed anyway. Turn the oven on to the lowest possible temperature; let it warm up and then turn it off. Place your botanicals on a cookie sheet (you might want to dedicate a cookie sheet to these projects, as some of your botanicals can leave a rather strong after-smell), and place it on the bottom of the oven.

Botanicals dry very quickly in the oven, so keep a close watch.

Mixing

Adding fragrance oils to the fixative maximizes the strength and longevity of the scent. As a guideline, use the following proportions when creating your own recipes: 15 to 20 drops of essential oil mixed with one tablespoon of orris root per each cup of botanicals (filler) you intend to mix. Gently mix the fixative–fragrance blend into your flowers, leaves, nuts, cones and other fillers. Remember that each element of the potpourri filler must be completely dried before they are mixed together. Ideally, use ceramic or glass bowls for mixing, and a metal spoon to mix.

Once the ingredients are well-integrated, place the mixture to rest in a sealed container (a large Mason-type jar is ideal) in a dark, dry place for about approximately one month, mixing it gently every other day. The best way to avoid damaging fragile elements during the mixing is to gently move it from jar to bowl and back.

Storing Extra Dried Flowers

Always keep your dried materials in airtight containers in warm and darkplaces. Exposure to light can change coloration and any exposure to moisture can lead to rot. Add a bit of silica gel ($^1/_2$ teaspoon per cup of filler) to ward off any potential dampness. Make sure there are no holes in the box you use to store your materials in; insects really like the cozy and aromatic atmosphere of a potpourri. Keep like materials together to avoid mixing scents, and remember to label each one. For example, flowers should be kept in one box, pine cones in another, etc. Large flower heads should be wrapped individually in tissue paper. If you are layering them in a box, always face the heads in the same direction so you'll know how to place your box.

Displaying

Never overlook this critical element of your overall design. The container for your potpourri is an important design element, and can be chosen for style, size, color or material.

Potpourri should be in an open container, so that the aroma can be released into the room. Jars, bowls or boxes that can be covered offer an added bonus; covering the mix when not in use will preserve the scent and the color. Glass, ceramic, wood, and even plastic are good materials to look for.

Baskets are pretty, but not practical, as small bits of your mix will leak out. However, try lining a basket with a colorful finely woven fabric, adding an additional customized element to your blends. For example, try a holiday print with green and red for Christmas blends, a remnant of delicate silk or chintz for the bedroom, or a seashell print or bandana for a casual look in a bathroom. Decorated cardboard boxes should be lined with elegant tissue paper or fabric. Some of those decorative ceramic bowls you might have received as gifts and forgotten in the kitchen cupboard can be perfect. Or collect flea market treasures and yard sale finds for future use. (Note: Try to avoid metal containers. These can cause a chemical reaction with dried botanicals, fixatives and oils that might alter the fragrance.) The container used for display can complement the mixture and add to its personality. Try a lacquered red basket for an oriental or spicy mixture, a wooden bowl for a classic country mix, a bright brass bowl for bold combinations of yellows and purples, or an interesting contemporary shape for a potpourri containing more non-traditional architectural elements. Shells can be perfect; try to find a curvy Nautilus shell, or a large scallop. In the bedroom, romantic or feminine crystal is appropriate.

Your potpourri can be an added touch anywhere–the top of a piano, a coffee table, windowsill, bookshelf.

Other Fragrant Crafts & Uses For Dried Flowers

If you have developed an interest and enthusiasm for this area of crafting, you might want to explore some additional uses for dried botanicals. Use extra potpourri mixtures to create sachets, linen bags, closet hangers or shoe stuffers. A tiny piece of fabric can turn a bit of your creation into a wonderful gift. Even the leftover dust from a particular favorite batch can be sprinkled on the bottom of a drawer or closet to sweeten the air. A practical and charming use of a hops-based mix is to create a sleep pillow stuffed with the mixture. Dried flowers are wonderful to add to your holiday or birthday gifts. Tie bunches of the flowers with pretty ribbons and nametags and place them at each place setting instead of an ordinary placeholder.

Preserving Your Potpourri

Try to keep your potpourri out of direct sunlight, as dried flowers and other botanicals can lose their color over time. Covering the potpourri display helps to preserve fragrance. Remember to "freshen" your mixture periodically (every 4 to 6 months) by adding a few drops of essential oil and blending well.

Potpourri Recipes

Here are some potpourri recipes for you to try at home. They are arranged in six categories: Floral, Woodsy, Mood Enhancing, Holiday, Fruity and Oriental/Exotic. Floral recipes include traditionally-inspired mixes that use flower petals, buds, and heads as their main ingredient, and sweet, floral fragrances. Delicate and fragrant leaves balance aroma and provide a backdrop for vivid color. Floral recipes are perfect for your own home, and also make wonderful house gifts when packaged in pretty containers.

Included in the mood enhancing section are potpourris whose base includes ingredients that are reputed to be restful, energizing, or stimulating. For centuries man has known of the powers of herbs and aroma; these mixes use that power and add a decorative element.

Holiday and seasonal mixes contain ingredients that have always been associated with particular holidays, and layer fragrant cues upon that. For Mother's Day and Valentine's Day, roses provide the feminine palette, and floral oils the fragrance. For December holidays, botanicals associated with the season, and festive decorations are used. Thanksgiving provides a slew of traditional materials for potpourri makers to work with.

Fruity mixes are fresh: citrus feature pretty slices of colorful fruits, whole fruits and citrus essences, and our fall fruit mix is a

floral

mood enhancing

woodsy/spicy

fruity

oriental/exotic

holiday/seasonal

homey blend of rich apples and pears. Finally, oriental/exotic mixes contain spices as a bold aromatic overtone, exotic flowers and pretty accents.

Experiment with these recipes. Try substituting elements to reach your own perfect mix. Use elements that you have picked and prepared yourself, or choose from the wondrous array of dried materials offered by potpourri suppliers. Explore unusual ingredients and containers. Almost any flower, leaf, petal, fruit or berry can be dried. Try to mix your own fragrances, too. Creating a personal fragrance can be your very own aromatic signature.

A Nor'eastern Late Spring

This exuberant and colorful floral mix is a vivid and fragrant reminder of bright springs days. The overall tones are oranges and yellows with a dash of deep purple.

Ingredients

- 3 CUPS HIBISCUS HEADS
(deep purple and yellow flowers)
- I CUP MARIGOLD HEADS (deep orange)
- ½ CUP KESU FLOWERS
- ½ CUPS WHITE ORCHID PETALS
- 2 CUP GREEN SHEET MOSS

- 4 DROPS GERANIUM ESSENTIAL OIL
- 2 DROPS ROSE ESSENTIAL OIL
- I DROP VANILLA OIL

Twisted Traditionals

This recipe features two classic potpourri ingredients—lavender and rose. Here, however, a modern twist has been added—a dramatic contrasting splash of chile peppers for color and spice.

Ingredients

- 2 CUPS LAVENDER FLOWERS
- 2 CUPS ROSE PETALS
- 2 CUPS LARKSPUR
- 1 CUPS LEMON SCENTED GERANIUM LEAVES
- 1 CUP HOPS
- 1/2 CUP LEMON PEEL IN SPIRALS OR TINY SQUARES
- A HANDFUL OF CHILE PEPPERS

- 5 DROPS LEMON OIL
- 8 DROPS LAVENDER OIL
- 2 TABLESPOONS OF ORRISROOT

Luxurious Summer

Orchids make a particularly festive and elegant floral base. The pastel tones and deep fragrances represent the best of what the summer has to offer. This lush recipe is perfect for presenting to your hosts on a summer weekend, displayed in small silver dish.

Ingredients

- 2 CUPS ORCHIDS
- 2 CUP PEONY PETALS
- I CUP SUNFLOWER PETALS
- I CUP WOODRUFF LEAVES
- I CUP FERN SPRIGS AS BACKDROP

- 3 TBS ORRISROOT CHUNKS
- 5 SILICA DRIED ORCHIDS AS ACCENT ON TOP
- 5 DROPS LILY OF THE VALLEY ESSENCE, OR ANY OTHER HEADY FLORAL ESSENCE
- 2 DROPS GINGER OIL

Vibrant Violet

Bursts of purples, reds and pinks with a fresh apple-toned scent make this blend a particularly bright potpourri, ideal for guest rooms and sitting rooms.

Ingredients

- 2 CUPS ORCHID PETALS
- I CUP GLOBE AMARANTH
- I CUP HIBISCUS
- I CUP PINK ROSEBUD PETALS
- I CUP OAK MOSS
- $^1\!/_2$ CUP JUNIPER BERRIES

- 8 DROPS APPLE OIL

Autumn Memories

The ingredients for this recipe can be gathered as you walk along a country path at peak leaf-changing season in the fall. Collect materials based on their color, shape and texture. An exotic blend of oils makes this a warm and sensual mix, with earthy undertones.

Ingredients

- 2 CUPS BRIGHTLY COLORED AUTUMN LEAVES
- 1 CUP MIXED ACORNS, NUTS, SEEDS AND PINECONES FROM A WOODLAND WALK
- 1 CUP GREEN SHEET MOSS
- 1 CUP ORANGE AND YELLOW FLOWER PETALS
- $^{1}/_{2}$ CUP BIRCH BARK
- $^{1}/_{2}$ CUP CEDAR CURLS

- 3 TABLESPOONS ORRIS ROOT
- 2 DROPS SANDALWOOD OIL
- 2 DROPS CEDAR OIL

Fragrant Forest

Pretty yellows and woodsy notes make this mix an ideal complement to any country living room.

Ingredients

- 2 CUPS YARROW
- 2 CUPS BALSAM NEEDLES
- I CUP TILIA
- I CUP CEDAR SHAVINGS
- I CUP UVA URSI
- I/4 CUP CINNAMON CHIPS
- I/4 CUP STAR ANISE

- 2 TABLESPOONS GUM BENZOIN

Breathe Deeply – A Fresh Eucalyptus Medley

Fresh, tangy and green. The eucalyptus leaves and surprising citrus twist give this recipe a non-traditional edge.

Ingredients

- 3 CUPS EUCALYPTUS LEAVES
- 2 CUPS BAY LEAVES
- 1 CUP ROSEMARY NEEDLES
- 1 CUP MIXED BARKS, SHREDDED INTO TINY PIECES
- 1 CUP WHOLE WHITE GLOBE AMARANTH FLOWERS
- 1 CUP HOPS FLOWERS
- 1 CUP SMALL HEMLOCK CONES
- 1 CUP LIME SLICED INTO SLENDER PEELS

- 5 DROPS LIME OIL
- 5 DROPS JUNIPER OIL
- 2 DROPS CLOVE OIL

Sweet Sweet Dreams

This recipe is comprised of ingredients that are each legendary for their soporific effects. It is said that George I himself regularly had a similar mix made up for his sleeping quarters.

Ingredients

- 2 CUPS HOPS
- 1 CUP LAVENDER
- 1 CUP DRIED LEMON VERBENA LEAVES
- 2 TABLESPOONS, GROUND ORRISROOT
- 2 DROPS LAVENDER OIL
- 1 DROP LEMON BALM OIL

Energy Boosting

Pine and peppermint each lend an invigorating snap to this mix.

Ingredients

- 1 CUP PINE NEEDLES
- 2 CUPS MIXED DRIED HERBS INCLUDING
- PEPPERMINT, BAY LEAF, THYME, BASIL AND
- ROSEMARY
- 1 CUP DRIED YARROW BLOSSOMS
- CHUNKS FROM LEMON PEEL

- 3 TABLESPOONS ORRISROOT CHIPS
- 2 DROPS BAY OIL
- 2 DROPS PEPPERMINT OIL

An Inspired Romantic

This recipe uses traditional fragrances long believed to hold powers to attract the opposite sex. Musk is an animal based scent, derived from the gland of a musk deer. Modern fragrance suppliers offer synthetic musk scents that give off the same earthy, rich and sensuous feeling.

Ingredients

- 6 CUPS DARK RED ROSE PETALS
- 2 CUPS PINK ROSEBUDS
- 2 CUPS ARTEMISIA LEAVES
- 1 CUP BABY'S BREATH
- 3 CUPS OAKMOSS
- 4 DROPS ROSE OIL
- 4 DROPS LILY OF THE VALLEY OIL
- 4 DROPS MUSK OIL
- 1 DROP VANILLA OIL

A Mother's Love

This blend, which includes some of the most classic potpourri ingredients, is a wonderful and simple way to say thank you to any mom on Mother's Day, or on any other day.

Ingredients

- 2 CUPS ROSE PETALS
- 1 CUP LAVENDER
- 1/2 CUP LEMON BALM LEAVES
- 1/2 CUP CHAMOMILE FLOWERS
- 2 TABLESPOONS ORRIS ROOT CHIPS

- 2 DROPS ROSE OIL
- 2 DROPS LAVENDER OIL

Be Sweet, Be True –
A Valentine's Day Potpourri

Lavish, and delightfully colorful romantic roses set the stage for a heady and rich fragrance. Use a varied palette of both roses and rosebuds, including creams, reds and pinks. No doubt a mixture pleasing to the eye as it is to the heart.

Ingredients

- 2 CUPS ROSEBUDS IN MIXED COLORS
- 3 CUPS ROSE PETALS IN MIXED COLORS
- $1/2$ CUP PATCHOULI LEAVES
- $1/2$ CUP DRIED MARJORAM LEAVES

- 2 TABLESPOONS ORRISROOT CHIPS
- 2 DROPS ROSE OIL
- 1 DROP JASMINE OIL

Give Thanks

Classical elements from Thanksgiving holidays in rich fall tones accent this beautiful and evocative potpourri. Herbs and spices redolent of home cooking make it good enough to want to eat.

Ingredients

- 2 CUPS SAGE LEAVES
- 2 CUPS BASIL LEAVES
- 2 CUPS INDIAN CORN KERNELS
- 2 CUPS ORANGE AND YELLOW FLOWER PETALS
- THIN SLICES FROM ONE ORANGE
- 1 CUP ACORNS
- 1 CUP CRANBERRIES
- 1 CUP OAKMOSS

- 5 DROPS GINGER OIL
- 5 DROPS NEROLI ESSENCE
- 1 DROP BAY OIL

December Cheer –
Family Holiday Mix

Textural variances combined with clear aromatic and visual cues make this holiday recipe a fragrant addition to your December hearth. Experiment with non-botanical elements for a personalized version: Gold powder is a festive addition to holiday mixes; tie a gold ribbon around some cinnamon sticks and use them as a finishing decorative touch; or place small gold Christmas balls next to the pomegranates for some added sparkle.

Ingredients

- 6 SMALL PINE CONES
- 4 LARGE HOLLY LEAVES
- 4 CINNAMON STICKS
- 2 CUPS EVERGREEN SPRIGS
- $1/2$ OAKMOSS
- $1/2$ CUP BAYBERRY LEAVES
- $1/4$ CUP CINNAMON CHIPS
- $1/8$ CUP ALLSPICE BERRIES
- $1/8$ CUP CRUSHED NUTMEG

- 4 DROPS SPRUCE OIL

Citrus Circus

This wonderful blend brings the fresh scent of summer indoors. A slight hint of floral fragrance helps to soften its overall tone. Yellows and greens are highlighted by orange bursts.

Ingredients

- 2 CUPS LEMON VERBENA LEAVES
- 1 $^1/_2$ CUPS DRIED LEMON PEEL, CUT
- 1 CUP DRIED LEMON GRASS
- 4 WHOLE LEMON SLICES
- 4 WHOLE LIME SLICES
- $^1/_2$ CUP DRIED LIME PEEL IN TINY PIECES
- $^1/_2$ CUP DRIED ORANGE PEEL IN TINY PIECES
- $^1/_2$ CUP MARIGOLD FLOWERS
- $^1/_2$ CUP TINY WHITE BLOSSOMS

- 5 DROPS MARIGOLD OIL
- 5 DROPS LIME OIL
- 5 DROPS LEMON OIL
- 2 TABLESPOONS ORRIS ROOT CHIPS

The Fruits of Fall

The comforting aroma of fruits and spices make this a wonderful year-round potpourri. Gather and dry your materials in the fall to make a big batch of this interesting composition.

Ingredients

- 3 CUPS DRIED APPLE SLICES
- 2 CUPS MEDIUM SIZED GREEN LEAVES
- 2 CUPS OAK MOSS
- $\frac{1}{2}$ CUP DRIED PEAR SLICES
- $\frac{1}{4}$ CUP CRUSHED CINNAMON
- $\frac{1}{4}$ CUP CRUSHED VANILLA BEANS
- $\frac{1}{2}$ CUP WHOLE CLOVES

Hot and Spicy Oranges

Warm tones of orange give this non-traditional mix a glowing look. The intense citrus aroma with a hint of clove will fill the room with warm, sensual desire.

Ingredients

- 4 WHOLE SMALL DRIED ORANGES
- 2 CUPS CHINESE LANTERNS
- 2 CUPS ORANGE PEEL, CUT INTO SPIRALS
- 2 CUPS ORANGE BLOSSOMS
- 1 CUP WHOLE NUTMEGS
- 1 CUP BOXWOOD LEAVES
- ½ CUP STAR ANISE

- 3 TABLESPOONS ORRISROOT
- 1 NUTMEG, GRATED
- 1 TSP GROUND CLOVES

- 10 DROPS GINGER OIL
- 10 DROPS ORANGE OIL

Jasmine Delight

Jasmine is heady in scent, and luxurious in feeling. Try this delightful and bold mix in the bedroom. Display it in an oriental ceramic container.

Ingredients

- 3 CUPS JASMINE PETALS
- 2 CUPS ROSE BUDS
- ½ CUP HIBISCUS FLOWERS
- ½ CUP MYRRH
- ¼ CUP CRUMBLED CINNAMON
- ¼ CUP SANDALWOOD CHIPS
- 1 STAR ANISE
- CRUSHED ORANGE PEEL,
  CUT INTO THIN STRIPS

- 3 DROPS JASMINE OIL
- 2 DROPS SANDALWOOD OIL
- 1 DROP ROSE OIL

Exotica

The exotic oils used in this pretty potpourri add to its overall appeal; be instantly transported by the luxurious heady aroma.

Ingredients

- 4 CUPS MIXED WHITE AND YELLOW FLOWER PETALS,
- USE WHATEVER YOU HAVE
- 2 CUPS SCENTED GERANIUM LEAVES
- I CUP OAKMOSS
- I / 2 CUP ROSE HIPS

- I TEASPOON CLOVES
- I DROP PATCHOULI OIL
- 2 DROPS YLANG-YLANG OIL
- 2 DROPS NARCISSUS OIL
- 2 TABLESPOONS ORRISROOT POWDER

- If you made or bought a large quantity of dried fruit, keep it in a cool place (even the refrigerator or freezer) during the summer. This helps keep away insects or moths.

- When drying flowers or herbs on stems, hang them around your kitchen or craft room—that way, you can keep an eye on them as they dry, and they add a lovely decorative effect to a room.

- Store leftover botanicals and fruits in separate sealed plastic bags: They'll keep for a long time, but their aromas can mingle and fade if they're stored together.

- For a quick and easy way to scent your living room, try applying essential oil to a pretty basket of pinecones that you have gathered on walks; adding a few drops will turn your decorative collection into a fragrant and simple potpourri!

- Label your boxes of drying materials, and do not mix materials in the boxes—they dry at different rates and aromas can mix

- To add sparkle to potpourri, try mixing in beads, sequins or even little pieces of ribbon or small toys—you can personalize your mixture in many unique and fun ways.

Essentials

Essential Oils

Essential oils are natural substances that are extracted from grasses, flowers, herbs, shrubs, trees, resins and spices, usually through a process called steam distillation. Oils can soothe, relax, rejuvenate, heal, energize or relieve pain, thereby affecting the body's physical, psychological and emotional levels. The use of oils in this manner is what is traditionally called aromatherapy.

SAFETY TIPS

- Essential oils should be stored in amber glass bottles away from direct sunlight and in a cool place. Never store an essential oil in a plastic bottle.
- If you store oils in the refrigerator, place the bottles in air-tight containers so that the aroma does not permeate food.
- Certain oils may solidify in cold temperatures due to their high wax content. If this occurs, place the oil bottle in a bowl of hot water to liquefy before use.
- Most essential oils have a shelf life of two years, with the exception of pine and citrus oils which lose some of their potency after 6 months.
- The color of certain oils may change with time; this does not affect the potency of the oil.
- Avoid using essential oils around the eye area.
- Never apply an essential oil directly to the skin; dilute it first (see below for dilution rates).
- Never use internally unless under the supervision and care of a specialist.
- Essential oils are not recommended for babies and small children and should always be stored out of the reach of children.

The following is a chart of the most essential of the essential oils and a brief description of their properties. Oils can be purchased at health food stores or by mail order.

NAME / LATIN NAME	PROPERTIES & SAFETY PRECAUTIONS
Ajowan *Trachyspermum copticum*	improves circulation, alleviates muscle pain • *use sparingly on sensitive skin*
Angelica *Angelica archangelica*	strengthening, restorative, anchoring • *avoid use in sun*
Aniseed *Pimpinella anisum*	aids in cramping, indigestion or digestive problems • *do not use if pregnant*
Armoise *Artimisia alba*	muscle relaxant, emollient • *do not use if pregnant*
Basil *Ocimum basilicum*	soothing agent, muscle relaxant, toning • *use sparingly*
Bay *Pimenta racemosa*	stimulating, energizing • *can cause skin irritation*
Bergamot *Citrus bergamia*	skin conditioner, soothing agent, antiseptic • *phototoxic*
Birch Tar *Betula lenta*	muscle relaxant, soothing agent • *do not use if pregnant*
Black Currant Seed *Ribes nigrum*	relieves PMS, high source of vitamin C
Black Pepper *Piper nigrum*	muscle relaxant
Cabreuva *Myocarpus fastigiatus*	calming, increases alertness
Cajeput *Melaleuca cajuputi*	stimulating, mood improving, antiseptic
Camphor *Cinnamon camphor*	soothing agent, conditioner, muscle relaxant • *do not use if pregnant or epileptic*
Cananga *Cananga odorata*	skin conditioner, deodorant
Caraway *Carum carvi*	muscle relaxant • *slight dermal toxicity*
Cardamom *Elettaria cardamomum*	muscle relaxant, skin conditioner, soothing agent
Carrot Seed *Daucus carota*	muscle relaxant, soothing agent, skin conditioner
Cedarwood Virginia *Juniperis virginiana*	antiseptic, skin conditioner, deodorant, soothing agent
Celery Seed *Apium graveolens*	toner
Chamomile Moroc *Anthemis mixta*	muscle relaxant, skin conditioner
Chamomile Roman *Anthemis noblis*	muscle relaxant, skin conditioner
Cinnamon Bark *Cinnamomum zeylanicum*	skin conditioner, anti-inflammatory agent • *can cause skin irritation*
Citronella *Cymbopogon nardus*	skin conditioner, insect repellent
Clary Sage *Salvia sclarea*	skin conditioner, astringent, soothing agent, muscle relaxant • *do not use if pregnant; do not drink alcohol or drive*
Clove Bud *Syzgium aromaticum*	muscle relaxant, soothing agent • *can cause skin irritation*
Copaiba Balsam *Copaifera officinalis*	increases circulation, reduces stress

Coriander *Corriandrum sativum*	muscle relaxant, soothing agent • *use sparingly*
Costus Root *Sassuriea costus*	calming
Cumin *Cuminum cyminum*	stimulating • *can cause skin irritation*
Cypress *Cupressus sempervirens*	antiseptic, astringent, soothing agent, skin conditioner • *flammable*
Cypriol *Cyperus scariosus*	aids digestion
Eucalyptus *Eucalyptus globulus* insect repellent	antiseptic, soothing agent, skin conditioner,
Evening Primrose *Centhera biennis*	good for dry skin and eczema
Fennel (sweet) *Foeniculum vulgare dulce*	muscle relaxant, soothing agent, antiseptic • *use sparingly*
Frankincense *Boswellia carteri*	skin conditioner, soothing agent
Galbanum *Ferula galbaniflua*	skin conditioner, muscle relaxant
Geranium *Pelargonium graveolen*	skin refresher, astringent
Ginger *Zingiber officinale*	astringent
Grapefruit *Citrus paradisi*	soothing agent, astringent, skin conditioner
Hyssop *Hyssopus officinalis*	soothing agent, skin conditioner • *do not use when pregnant, if suffering from* *epilepsy or high blood pressure*
Jasmine Absolute *Jasminum officinale*	emollient, soothing agent, antiseptic
Juniper *Juniperus communis*	skin detoxifier, astringent, soothing agent • *flammable*
Labdanum *Cistus ladanifer*	skin conditioner
Lavandin *Lavandula hybrida*	soothing agent, muscle relaxant, skin conditioner, astringent
Lavender *Lavandula officinalis*	muscle relaxant, skin conditioner, soothing agent, astringent
Lemon *Citrus limonum*	soothing agent, antiseptic
Lemongrass *Cymbopogon flexuosus*	skin conditioner, soothing agent, muscle relaxant, antiseptic • *can cause skin irritation*
Lime *Citrus aurantifolia*	soothing agent, skin conditioner, astringent
Mandarin *Citrus reticulata*	soothing agent, astringent, skin conditioner
Manuka *Leptospermum*	relieves aches and pains, healing to the skin
Marjoram *Origanum marjorana*	antiseptic, calming
Mimosa *Acacia dealbata*	muscle relaxant, skin conditioner, soothing agent
Myrrh *Commiphora myrrha*	anti-inflammatory agent, emollient, antiseptic • *use in moderation if pregnant*

NAME / LATIN NAME	PROPERTIES & SAFETY PRECAUTIONS
Myrtle *Myrtus communis*	soothing agent, astringent, skin conditioner, muscle relaxant
Neroli *Citrus aurantium*	antiseptic, emollient
Nutmeg Myristica fragrans *Niaouli elaleuca viridiflora*	antiseptic, soothes irritated skin, muscle relaxant • **use sparingly**
Orange *Citrus sinensis*	astringent, soothing agent, skin conditioner
Origanum *Origanum vulgare*	increases energy • **can cause skin irritation**
Palmarosa *Cymbopogon martini*	skin conditioner, soothing agent, emollient, muscle relaxant
Patchouli *Pogostemon cablin*	anti-inflammatory agent, antiseptic, astringent
Peppermint *Mentha arvensis*	emollient, antiseptic, muscle relaxant can cause skin irritation
Petitgrain *Petitgrain bigarade*	relieves anxiety and stress
Pine *Pinus sylvestris*	antiseptic • **can cause skin irritation**
Rose Absolute *Rosa damascena*	skin conditioner
Rose Otto *Rosa —*	astringent
Rosemary *Rosmarinus officinalis*	antiseptic, muscle relaxant, soothing agent, skin conditioner • **do not take if pregnant or have high blood pressure**
Rosewood *Aniba rosaeodora*	muscle relaxant
Sage *Dalmatian Salvia officinalis*	soothing agent • **do not use if pregnant or suffering from epilepsy**
Sandalwood *(Mysore) Sandalum album*	antiseptic, emollient, soothing agent, astringent, skin conditioner
Spearmint *Mentha spicata*	emollient, astringent, soothing agent, muscle relaxant • **use sparingly**
Tarragon *Artimisia dracunculus*	astringent
Tea Tree *Melaleuca alternifolia*	antiseptic • **may cause irritation to sensitive skin**
Thyme *Thymus vulgaris*	antiseptic, toner • **can cause skin irritation**
Vanilla *Vanilla planifolia*	emollient
Vetiver *Vetiveria zizanioides*	emollient, reduces blood pressure
Violet Leaves *Viola*	soothing agent, skin conditioner
Yarrow *Achillea millefolium*	reduces scarring
Ylang-Ylang *Cananga odorata*	reduces stress and tension
Zanthoxylum *Zanthoxylum alatum*	reduces stress and tension

ADDITIONAL CANDLE DECORATING IDEAS

Melt a small amount of high melting point paraffin wax in a saucepan and use it as you would glue to stick beads, decorative paper cut-outs or seashells to the exterior of your candles. Paint the melted wax onto the candle's surface with a small paintbrush and hold the object in place until the wax is completely dry. For pressed flowers or leaves, paint over the flower or leaf to further secure the item to the wax surface. Or try painting a delicate motif on your tapers, for example, using a sponge or paintbrush.

Remember to remove excess debris from wax pool after each use.

- Rhinestones
- Seeds (mustard, fennel, etc)
- Beads (plastic, glass or metal)
- Fake pearls
- Paints (acrylic, gouaches, poster paints)
- Marble chips
- Paper doilies
- Glitter
- Glitter glue
- Tissue paper
- Origami paper
- Confetti
- Wire (copper, silver)
- Seashells
- Pebbles
- Ribbon
- Stencils
- Stickers
- Decals
- String
- Burlap
- Dried leaves
- Dried flowers and petals
- Dried fruit and nuts
- Dried beans and lentils
- Grated lemon/lime/orange peel
- Potpourri
- Pieces of bark, pinecones, acorns
- Cinnamon sticks
- Vanilla beans
- Coffee beans
- Ground spices *(cinnamon, curry, cloves, nutmeg, cumin, red pepper flakes, etc)*

USING AND STORING CANDLES

- Place candles in a candle holder or plate to avoid damaging furniture surfaces.

- Melt a few drops of wax in the candle holder or plate before putting in candle to hold it in place.

- Keep out of direct sunlight to prevent warping, melting and fading

- Keep wicks trimmed to 1/4 inch before using

- Buff the surface of a scratched or dull candle with a piece of nylon stocking to give it shine and to remove dust.

- Add a drop of essential oil to the wax pool of a burning candle for additional aroma

- Keep burning candles out of drafts to prevent uneven burning, wax splatters, and dripping

- Keep curtains, dried flowers and all flammable objects away from burning candles

- Never let a candle burn down to the end. Blow it out when it gets to one inch from bottom.

- Avoid wax splashes by holding your hand behind the flame before blowing it out

- Never leave a burning candle unattended

- Wrap unused candles in a soft cloth or white tissue paper before storing

- Wrap scented candles in a plastic bag

- Store unused candles flat and in a cool, dark place

WAX SPILLS AND CLEAN UP

- Always cover your candle making area (counters and floors) with plastic garbage bags or wax paper. In case of a spill, let wax harden and peel off to reuse.

- Make sure that you are wearing appropriate clothing when making candles. Feet, hands, arms, and legs should be covered as much as possible.

- Clean out all candle making equipment as quickly as possible (before wax hardens) with paper towels or rags.

- For spilled wax on skin: immediately place the affected area under cold water. Once the wax is hard, carefully peel off the wax and treat the affected area as you would any other burn. Apply burn relief cream or aloe gel. If the affected area is larger than the size of a walnut, consult a doctor for further treatment.

- For spilled wax on carpet, upholstery or curtains: harden wax with ice and remove as much as you can with a dull knife. For any leftover wax, use a paper towel or brown paper bag as a blotter and run a warm iron over it to absorb the wax.

- For spilled wax on clothing: put the item of clothing in the freezer to harden wax, then scrape off as much as possible before applying a warm iron on a paper towel to absorb excess.

- Save unused wax, separate by color and wax type (beeswax v. paraffin, high melting point v. low melting point) and store in labeled plastic bags for future use.

GROWING YOUR OWN BOTANICALS

Growing flowers and leaves to use in potpourri is a wonderful way to extend the potpourri-making process. Fill your garden or window box with aromatic flowers and herbs, and your potpourris will be even more special and personalized!

PERENNIALS survive for at least 3 years; most last much longer. Garden flower perennials bloom on average for 2-3 weeks at a specific time during the year.

ANNUALS are plants that last one season, going through an entire life cycle during that time. Most prefer sun, and should be watered once a week in the absence of rain. Make sure to plant annuals after the last frost has passed.

BULBS are actually living containers concealing all the elements of the plant, which only appears for a few months.

BIENNIALS live for two years.

Wild Thyme

Chinese Lantern

Rosemary

Lavender

Chervil

NAME	TYPE	SEASON	CONDITIONS TO PICK
CARNATION	PERENNIAL	spring/summer	• well-drained soil, full sun
CORIANDER	ANNUAL	spring	• sunny, some shade, well-drained soil
DAISIES	PERENNIAL	fall	• full sun/fertile soil
DELPHINIUM	PERENNIAL	summer/early fall	• full sun, rich moist soil, well drained soil; Cut when bottom blooms are fully open, top buds just showing color
FOXGLOVE	BIENNIAL	late summer/fall	• part shade, acid soil, moist
FREESIA	BULBS	spring/summer	• warm days/cool nights; do best in warm climates
GERANIUM	ANNUAL	summer	• lots of sun, well drained soil, warm days, cool nights
GLOBE AMARANTH	ANNUAL	summer	• full sun, dry/sandy soil
HYDRANGEA	PERENNIAL	summer	• full sun or some shade • Moist soil with peat moss
HONESTY	BIENNIAL	spring	• partial shade
LAVENDER	PERENNIAL	spring/summer	• full sun, well-drained soil, cut as soon as buds begin to open
LARKSPUR	ANNUAL	late spring/summer	• full sun, well-drained rich soil
MARIGOLD	ANNUAL	summer/fall	• heavy sun, average moisture
OREGANO	PERENNIAL	summer	• shade, average moisture, harvest before full bloom
PEONY	PERENNIAL	summer	• full sun, moist rich soil
ROSE	ANNUAL	late spring/summer	• sunny, with some shade Fertile, moist soil
ROSEMARY	PERENNIAL	summer	• sunny, well-drained soil
STRAWFLOWER	ANNUAL		• full sun, sandy dryish soil
SUNFLOWER	ANNUAL	late summer/fall	• requires lots of sun and moisture
THYME	PERENNIAL	summer	• sunny area/sandy soil, harvest just before flowering
TULIP	BULB	spring/early summer	• rich soil/good drainage
YARROW	PERENNIAL	summer	• full sun dryish soil
ZINNIA	ANNUAL	summer/fall	• full sun, rich drained soil

HINTS & TIPS

- Try to collect plant material on a warm day, after the dew has evaporated, but before the sun is at its peak.

- You can use flowers at any stage buds, entire flowerheads or petals. Experiment with the various stages of each of your favorite flowers.

- Pick a few of the most perfect blooms from each batch of flowers and preserve them in silica. This makes the perfect decorative top note for your potpourri.

- Remember that botanicals take varying amounts of time to dry. Dry bunches of like materials together, no matter what method you are using.

- Make sure your flowers, herbs and plants are completely dry before mixing your recipe. Any moisture left can lead to mold. One good way to tell is to place them in a glass jar with a tight light. Leave the blooms for a couple of days; if you see any moisture, continue the drying process.

- Be inventive – even non-organic material can be used creatively in your potpourri projects. Think of glitter, confetti, sparkles or even beads for special occasions.

- When creating your own recipes, begin with a fragrance that is close to your primary ingredients, then layer additional scents on top, should you choose. Start with simple combinations of oils to learn what you like and what works well together.

- You can prepare your fragrances in advance by adding the oils to chunks of orris root and letting them age together. Have a number of oils ready and labeled to experiment with.

- Keep a notebook and pen at your side as you are creating your own mixtures. Note down proportions and ingredients.

- Let your mixture sit in a cool, dark place for at least 4 weeks and stir it each day.

- Never place your potpourri in bright light – it fades!

- You can cover the potpourri to prolong its scent

- When the scent begins to fade, you can add a touch of fragrance oil and/or spice to invigorate the mixture.

- Store-bought oils vary greatly in strength and scent, depending on your source. Experiment with different brands to find the perfect one for you.

- Keep leftover potpourri and even the potpourri dust. It is a wonderful basis for other scented crafts, including sachets, shoe stuffers, etc.

GLOSSARY OF TERMS AND TECHNIQUES

*=Words, terms and expressions commonly used in candle-making

•=Words, terms and expressions commonly used in making potpourri

- **Air-drying** a method of drying botanicals in preparation for their use in potpourri. Air-drying can consist of hanging bunches of like items, or laying the elements on drying trays, screens or flat baskets.

- **Aromatherapy** the art of using aromatic essences (essential oils) derived from flowers, leaves, roots, woods and fruits. These essences can be used for various therapeutic purposes including scenting potpourri, massage, inhalation therapy and baths. The word "aromatherapy" was first coined by the French in the 1930s.

- **Aromatic** having a scent or fragrance. Many leaves, flowers, barks and other botanical materials used in the making of potpourri do not maintain their fragrance once dried.

* **Beeswax** made by honeybees, beeswax is a golden yellowish wax that is usually mixed with paraffin for candlemaking purposes. Beeswax gives a sweet aroma to the wax, renders it more pliable (good for making rolled candles) and makes the candle burn longer. However, beeswax is sticky and will stick to molds.

* **Buff** to shine or remove scratches from the surface of a finished candle; can be done with a piece of pantyhose.

* **Burn Rate** rates the performance of a candle. Burn rate is determined by weighing the candle, burning it for a determined period of time, then re-weighing the candle including any wax that dripped. The burn rate will represent the amount of wax (in grams) burned or consumed per minute. The lower the burn rate of a candle, the longer it will last.

* **Casting** a candle making method in which a temporary or disposable form such as sand, clay, an egg shell, or a pumpkin serves as the mold. Candles made with the casting method are usually good for one use only.

- **Cellulose** a fixative, derived from ground corncobs. Cellulose is an effective fixative, especially popular with those that are prone to allergic reactions, commonly associated with orrisroot.

* **Clear Crystals** a wax additive that raises its melting point, thus increasing the candle's burning time. It also helps eliminate bubbles from the surface of the wax. Good for making hurricane candles.

- **Closet hangers** small, potpourri-filled sachets specifically designed to sweeten a closet. Often closet hangers are stuffed with a moth-repellent mix of herbs and flowers.

* **Container Candle** a "pouring process" candle in which the melted wax is poured into a container (glass jar, enamel pot, aluminum tin). The container becomes a part of the final candle.

* **Cored Wicks** a type of wick used primarily for making votives and container candles. It has a metal wire center which makes the wick stiff so tat it can stand on its own and not move around when the melted wax is poured.

- **Desiccant** a desiccant is a material that acts to quicken the drying process by absorbing the water naturally found in plants, flowers and herbs. Desiccants commonly used in preparing the elements used for potpourri include oakmoss, orrisroot, cellulose granules, sand and silica.

* **Dipped Candle** a candle that is made by repeatedly dipping a wick into melted wax, letting the wax cool and harden between dips. It takes about approximately 40 dips to make a dipped candle.

* **Dipping Frame** a piece of equipment necessary for making hand-dipped candles and tapers. The wick is attached to it at both ends, thus keeping it taught for dipping in the melted wax.

* **Dipping Vat** a piece of equipment that holds the melted wax in which the dipping frame is dipped.

* an old-fashioned term for a utensil that extinguishes a flame on a candle; now called a candle snuffer.

* **Drawn Candle** a modern candlemaking process which involves pulling wick through melted wax to make very thin candles such as birthday candles.

* **Embossing** imprinting the outer surface of the candle to make designs.

•* **Essential Oil** the purest form of fragrance that can be derived from flowers, fruits, leaves, etc. Oils such as jasmine, rose, bay or sandalwood are used to enhance the fragrance of potpourri. Essential oils are commercially available and can also be created at home using a basic distillation process. Essential oils are also used as the basis for aromatherapy.

• **Filler** the bulk, or basis of a potpourri mix, consisting of flower heads, buds, petals, leaves, grasses, cones, nuts, berries, woods, fruits, mushrooms and mosses. To the filler is added the fixative, the agent that acts to bind the fragrance to the botanicals and the essential or fragrance oil, which is the fragrance.

• **Fixative** a fixative is any material that helps 'fix' the fragrance onto the filler by efficiently absorbing and retaining the essential oils. There are secondary, or weaker, fixatives that include gum resins, such as myrrh, frankincense and benzoin, and some roots and seeds have fixative properties, too (coriander, vetiver). In the past, animal products have also been used as effective fixatives (ambergis, musk), but are rarely used currently. The most common fixatives used today are orrisroot, derived from the Iris florentina, oakmoss (a moss) and cellulose (derived from corncobs.)

* **Flash Point** the temperature at which a wax will catch on fire.

* **Flat Braid** a type of wick used primarily for making tapers or small pillar candles. It comes in different sizes (determined by the number of strands in the wick) to be determined by the type of candle desired.

• **Food Dehydrator** a kitchen appliance that is most commonly used to dry fruits, potpourri makers have discovered that dehydrators also work to dry botanical material.

•* **Fragrance** one of the three main components in the potpourri (the others being filler and fixative.) The fragrance component of potpourri is comprised of essential and fragrance oils, as well as the distinct aromas that certain botanical elements add (not all flowers add fragrance once dried.)

* **Hurricane Candle** a type of candle in which the outer shell is made of wax (usually combined with some decorative ingredient like dried fruit, flowers, or leaves) and the inside is left hollow and filled with wax or a votive candle. Only the inner candle — which can be replaced when finished — burns, leaving the outer shell intact.

• **Lichen** a moss-like substance made up of two co-existing organisms, algae and fungus. Lichen is often found growing on tree branches and is a lovely addition to potpourri mixes, adding a unique textural element and woodsy feeling. Oakmoss is a lichen and a widely used fixative.

• **Linen Bag** an herb and/or floral-filled sachet meant specifically to freshen a linen closet or drawer.

* **Luster Crystals** a wax additive that hardens wax and raises its melting point, thus making the candle last longer. It also improves the iridescence of the wax and brightens its color.

* **Melt Pool** the size of the pool of melted wax around the wick of a burning candle

* **Melting Point** the temperature at which wax melts. Different waxes have different

melting points.

* **Metal Core Wick** see Core Wick

• **Moist Potpourri** the forerunner to today's pot-pourris were jars containing fragrant combi-nations of flower petals (traditionally roses), spices and salts. Remarkably long-lasting (some moist potpourris last for decades), this method results in a rather gloomy-looking mixture (soggy, grayish liquid with lumps). This was really the original ërot potí.

* **Mold Release** spray used to treat a candle mold before the wax is poured that aids in unmolding the candle once it is cool.

* **Mold Sealer** putty that seals wick holes in molds.

* **Molten Wax** melted liquid wax.

* **Mordant** a fire-retardant solution used on wicks.

* **Mycrocrystalline Wax** a refined wax additive that increases the durability of a candle or adhesion or ìstickinessî of wax, useful for overdipping.

* **Novelty Candle** a less traditional type of candle that is irregularly shaped .

• **Oven drying** a drying method can be used effectively to dry certain leaves, herbs, or plant material. Oven drying botanicals must be closely attended, as the drying occurs quickly and can lead to burning.

* **Overdipping** a process by which candles are dipped into a wax with a higher melting point than the rest of the candle to make them drip-less. An exterior shell that burns slower than the wax inside is created. The melted wax inside combusts before it has a chance to drip. Also gives a nice finish to rolled candles.

* **Paraffin Wax** a by-product of the oil refining industry, paraffin is the most common candle-making wax. There are different types of paraffin wax, with different melting points high, medium and low.

* **Pillar Candle** a thick candle measured by the size of its diameter. Pillar candles can be round, square, oval, or hexagonal.

• **Pomander** a pomander is any hanging dried flower, herb/spice arrangement that is circular in shape. Pomanders were especially popular in Victorian times and were originally used to guard against infec-tions. Classic pomanders consist of a dried orange or other citrus fruit studded with cloves. Floral pomanders are fashioned by adhering dried flowers to a round shape, often foam, to create a unique decorative accessory.

• **Posy** a tiny personal bouquet, made up of dried flowers. Originally posies were used by ladies during the Victorian period and served to scent the dense and rank air of crowded urban areas. Posy now indicates any dried floral arrangement that is in the shape of a bouquet.

* **Poured Candle** a candle that is made by pouring melted wax into a mold or container

* **Pouring Temperature** temperature at which the wax should be when poured into a mold, container or when used for hand-dipping.

* **Pressed Candle** a candle made by pouring wax beads and pressing them into molds. Pressed candles are easier to remove from molds than candles made with molten wax.

* **Priming** prior to making a candle, the wick must be primed – or saturated with wax – to eliminate trapped air in the wick.

* **Rolled Candle** a candle that is made by rolling a sheet of beeswax or paraffin wax around a wick.

• **Sachets** small fabric packages or pillows containing potpourri. They are often used to freshen drawers or closets.

* **Sheet Wax** wax that is in sheet form; usually made out of pure beeswax but can be a beeswax and paraffin combination.

- **Silica** a mineral, whose highly absorbent crystal form is used as a desiccant (drying agent) for fresh botanicals. Silica-drying results in near-perfect dried flower forms. Silica crystals are easily found through potpourri suppliers. Many crystals have a color-indicating feature, indicating precisely when the botanicals are dry. The crystals can be recycled for repeated use by simply warming in the oven.

* **Snuffing** snipping the wick to prevent smoking.

* **Square Braid** a type of wick used primarily for making casted candles or large pillar candles.

* **Stearic Acid** a common candlemaking additive that lowers the melting point of paraffin wax and makes the final candle harder thus minimizing prevent braking and bending. It also helps make paraffin wax more opaque.

* **Synthetic Polymers** candlemaking additives that increase brilliance and translucence of wax, raise its melting point, make it more or less pliable and can also aid in mold release.

* **Tapers** long candles that have been traditionally made using the hand-dipping method. Tapers are generally between 3/4 inch and 7/8 inch in diameter at their base.

* **Votive Candle** a small candle made with a wire core wick and that stands on its own. Votive candles are usually no taller than 2 or 3 inches and can fit into small containers and spaces.

* **Whipped Wax** wax that has been beaten with a fork until it is foamy. Candles made with whipped wax look like cake icing or snow.

* **Wick Holder** holds wicks in place when making hand-dipped candles and tapers.

* **Wick Rod** a piece of equipment to which the wick is attached and that is placed above the top of the container. It holds the wick in place when the melted wax is being poured. A pencil, chopstick or piece of coathanger can do the trick.

* **Wick Tab** a small square or circle of soft metal in which a wick is inserted; wick tabs prevent the wick from moving around in the mold when the wax is being poured.

RESOURCES, SUPPLIERS AND MANUFACTURERS

USEFUL WEBSITES

Candles:

Candle Club
www.candle-club.com/

Candle Radiance
www.candleradiance.com/

The Candle Shop
www.the-candle-shop.com/

The Crowley Candle Factory
www.wholesalecandlesupply.com/

Candle Equipment and Supplies
www.waxmelters.com/

Candle Makers
sers.wantree.com.au/~campbell/prod.htm

Candle Making Tips
ansel.his.duq.edu/%7Edoughert/TIPS.HTM

The Pennsylvania Arts and Craft Emporium
www.demanddigital.com/supplies/candles/
candle.htm

Country Lane Candle Supplies
www.clcs.com

Lynder House International, Inc.
www.compusmart.ab.ca/sbra/lynden

Pourette Manufacturing
www.members.aa.net/~pourette/

Activa Products, Inc.
www.activa-products.com

Potpourri:

Herbs Depot (herbs, oils, spices, teas, leaves)
www.herbs-depot.com

Motherlove Herbs (herbs and oils)
www.motherlove.com

Natures Bouquet (oils)
www.naturesbouquet.com

The Flower Mart (flowers, grasses, leaves)
www.theflowermart.com
The Herb Peddler (herbs)
www.thefoodstores.com

Aroma World (essential oils)
www.aromaworld.com

Atlantic Spice Co.
(herbs, spices, oils, nuts, seeds) www.
Atlanticspice.com

Essential Essences (oils)
www.essentialessences.com

SUPPLIERS

Candles:

Pearl Paint
308 Canal Street
New York, NY 10013
(212) 41-7932

Pourette Manufacturing, Inc.
1418 Northwest 53rd Street
Seattle, WA 98107
(800) 888-9425

Candleshtick (2 locations)
2444 Broadway
New York, NY 10024-1103
(212)787-5444

181 7th Ave.
New York, NY 10011
(212)924-5444

Lynden House International, Inc.
P.O. Box 69033
13915-127 Street
Edmonton, Alberta T5I 4Z8
Canada
(403) 448-0072

Candle Maker's Supplies
28 Blythe Road
London, W14 0HA
England
(071) 602-4031

The Candle Mill
Old Mill Road
East Arlington, VT 05252
(800) 772-3759

Activa Products
Box 472
Westford, MA 01886-0012
(978) 692-9300
(800) 255-1910

General Wax & Candle Co.
800-WAX-STORE

Yankee Candle Company
800-243-1776

The Hearthsong Catalog
800-325-2502

Potpourri:

Aphrodisia (oils, books)
282 Bleecker Street, New York, NY 10014, (212) 989-6440

Floral Home (flowers, branches, grasses)
5400 Scotts Valley Drive
Scotts Valley, CA 95066
800-622-7372
www.floralhome.com

San Francisco Herb Peddler (herbs)
250 14th street
San Francisco, CA 94103
1 (800)-227-4530
www.sfherb.com

Sluderfloral.com (flowers, leaves, fruit, moss)
6900 Linville Falls Highway
Newland, NC 28657
1 (800) 438-6047
www.sluderfloral.com

Swissette Herb Farm (herbs)
216 Clove Road
Salisbury Mills, NY, 12577,
914-496-7841
www.meadownet.com/swissette

CRAFT ASSOCIATIONS

American Institute of Floral Design
410-752-3318
www.aifd.org

The American Herbal Products Association
www.ahpa.com

Crafts Designers
(740) 452-4541
www.creativeindustries.com

Cut Flowers Association
(440) 774-2887
www. Ascfg.org

Hobby Association of American
(201) 794-1133
www.hobby.org

National Crafts Association
(800) 7`5-9584
www.craftsassoc.com

The Herb Growing and Marketing Network
www.herbnet.com

BIBLIOGRAPHY

Black, Penny. *The Scented House*. London: Dorling Kindersley Limited, 1990

Blacklock, Judith. *Teach Yourself Dried Flowers*. Chicago: NTC Publishing Group, 1993

Blake, Jane and Paulsen, Emily. *Handmade Candles*. New York: Hearst Books, 1998

Coney, Norma. *The Complete Candlemaker*. North Carolina: Lark Books, 1997

Gips, Kathleen M., ed. *The Language of Flowers: A Book of Victorian Sentiments*. Chagrin Falls, OH: Pine Creek Herbs, 1990

Hillier, Malcolm. *Decorating with Dried Flowers*. London, Dorling Kindersley Limited, 1987

Ishaque, Labeena. *Heaven Scent*. New York: Watson Guptill Publications, 1998

Keller, Erich. *The Complete Home Guide to Aromatherapy*. Tiburon, California: H J Kramer, Inc., 1991

Larkin, Chris. *The Book of Candlemaking*. New York: Sterling Publishing Co., Inc., 1998

Lawless, Julia. *The Illustrated Encyclopedia of Essential Oils*. Dorset: Element Books, 1995

Lipari, Paul. *The Essence of Aromatherapy*. Kansas City: Ariel Book, 1998

Ohrbach, Barbara M. *The Scented Room*. New York: Clarkson Potter, 1986

Oppenheimer, Betty. *The Candlemaker's Companion*. Vermont: Storey Books, 1997

Randolph, Barbara. *Potpourri*. New York: Crescent Books, 1991

Rippin, Joan. *Potpourri and Scented Gifts*. New York: Lorenz Books, 1997

Shaudys, Phyllis V. *Herbal Treasures*. Vermont: Storey Communications, 1990

Sheen, Joanna. *Potpourri, Creating Long Lasting Natural Fragrance for the Home*. London: Ward Lock, 1992

Williams, Betsy. *Potpourri and Fragrant Crafts*. New York: Reader's Digest Association, Inc., 1996

INDEX

PAMPER YOURSELF WITH
THE OTHER TITLES IN THE
LIFE'S LITTLE LUXURIES SERIES

Author Catherine Bardey shows you how to revitalize
and aromatize your skin and hair or create a relaxing
oasis of serenity, comfort or romance in your home.
Whether it's your body or mind, these books show
you how to relax, rejuvenate and simply treat yourself
right—and you deserve it!

SECRETS OF THE SPAS, $10.98

ISBN 1-57912-063-6

MAKING CANDLES & POTPOURRI, $10.98

ISBN 1-57912-094-6

ALL TITLES ARE AVAILABLE AT YOUR FAVORITE BOOKSTORE OR ONLINE